APPRECIATIONS AND CRITICISMS OF THE WORKS OF CHARLES DICKENS

BY

G. K. CHESTERTON

KENNIKAT PRESS, INC./PORT WASHINGTON, N. Y.

APPRECIATIONS AND CRITICISMS OF THE WORKS OF CHARLES DICKENS

Copyright 1911 by E.P. Dutton and Company
Reissued in 1966 by Kennikat Press

Library of Congress Catalog Card No: 66-21382

CONTENTS

Contents

Criticisms and Appreciations

INTRODUCTION

THESE papers were originally published as prefaces
to the separate books of Dickens in one of the most
extensive of those cheap libraries of the classics which
are one of the real improvements of recent times.
Thus they were harmless, being diluted by, or rather
drowned in Dickens. My scrap of theory was a mere
dry biscuit to be taken with the grand tawny port of
great English comedy; and by most people it was not
taken at all—like the biscuit. Nevertheless the essays
were not in intention so aimless as they appear in fact.

I had a general notion of what needed saying about
Dickens to the new generation, though probably I did
not say it. I will make another attempt to do so in this
prologue, and, possibly fail again.

There was a painful moment (somewhere about the
eighties) when we watched anxiously to see whether
Dickens was fading from the modern world. We have
watched a little longer, and with great relief we begin to
realise that it is the modern world that is fading. All
that universe of ranks and respectabilities in comparison
with which Dickens was called a caricaturist, all that
Victorian universe in which he seemed vulgar—all that
is itself breaking up like a cloudland. And only the

caricatures of Dickens remain like things carved in
stone. This, of course, is an old story in the case of a
man reproached with any excess of the poetic. Again
and again when the man of visions was pinned by the
sly dog who knows the world,

> "The man recovered of the bite,
> The dog it was that died."

To call Thackeray a cynic, which means a sly dog,
was indeed absurd; but it is fair to say that in comparison with Dickens he felt himself a man of the world.
Nevertheless, that world of which he was a man is coming to an end before our eyes; its aristocracy has grown
corrupt, its middle class insecure, and things that he
never thought of are walking about the drawing-rooms
of both. Thackeray has described for ever the Anglo-
Indian Colonel; but what on earth would he have done
with an Australian Colonel? What can it matter
whether Dickens's clerks talked cockney now that half
the duchesses talk American? What would Thackeray
have made of an age in which a man in the position of
Lord Kew may actually be the born brother of Mr.
Moss of Wardour Street? Nor does this apply merely
to Thackeray, but to all those Victorians who prided
themselves on the realism or sobriety of their descriptions; it applies to Anthony Trollope and, as much
as any one, to George Eliot. For we have not only
survived that present which Thackeray described: we
have even survived that future to which George Eliot
looked forward. It is no longer adequate to say that
Dickens did not understand that old world of gentility,

of parliamentary politeness and the balance of the constitution. That world is rapidly ceasing to understand itself. It is vain to repeat the complaint of the old Quarterly Reviewers, that Dickens had not enjoyed a university education. What would the old Quarterly Reviewers themselves have thought of the Rhodes Scholarships? It is useless to repeat the old tag that Dickens could not describe a gentleman. A gentleman in our time has become something quite indescribable.

Now the interesting fact is this: That Dickens, whom so many considered to be at the best a vulgar enthusiast, saw the coming change in our society much more soberly and scientifically than did his better educated and more pretentious contemporaries. I give but one example out of many. Thackeray was a good Victorian radical, who seems to have gone to his grave quite contented with the early Victorian radical theory—the theory which Macaulay preached with unparalleled luminosity and completeness; the theory that true progress goes on so steadily through human history, that while reaction is indefensible, revolution is unnecessary. Thackeray seems to have been quite content to think that the world would grow more and more liberal in the limited sense; that Free Trade would get freer; that ballot boxes would grow more and more secret; that at last (as some satirist of Liberalism puts it) every man would have two votes instead of one. There is no trace in Thackeray of the slightest consciousness that progress could ever change its direction. There is in Dickens. The whole of *Hard Times* is the expression of just such a realisation. It is not true to say that Dickens was a Socialist, but it is not absurd

to say so. And it would be simply absurd to say it
of any of the great Individualist novelists of the Victorian time. Dickens saw far enough ahead to know
that the time was coming when the people would be
imploring the State to save them from mere freedom,
as from some frightful foreign oppressor. He felt
the society changing; and Thackeray never did.

As talking about Socialism and Individualism is
one of the greatest bores ever endured among men,
I will take another instance to illustrate my meaning,
even though the instance be a queer and even a delicate
one. Even if the reader does not agree with my de-
duction, I ask his attention to the fact itself, which I
think a curiosity of literature. In the last important
work of Dickens, that excellent book *Our Mutual
Friend*, there is an odd thing about which I cannot make
up my mind; I do not know whether it is unconscious
observation or fiendish irony. But it is this. In *Our
Mutual Friend* is an old patriarch named Aaron, who
is a saintly Jew made to do the dirty work of an abominable Christian usurer. In an artistic sense I think
the patriarch Aaron as much of a humbug as the
patriarch Casby. In a moral sense there is no doubt
at all that Dickens introduced the Jew with a philanthropic idea of doing justice to Judaism, which he was
told he had affronted by the great gargoyle of Fagin.
If this was his motive, it was morally a most worthy
one. But it is certainly unfortunate for the Hebrew
cause that the bad Jew should be so very much more
convincing than the good one. Old Aaron is not an
exaggeration of Jewish virtues; he is simply not Jewish
because he is not human. There is nothing about him

that in any way suggests the nobler sort of Jew, such a man as Spinoza or Mr. Zangwill. He is simply a public apology, and like most public apologies, he is very stiff and not very convincing.

So far so good. Now we come to the funny part. To describe the high visionary and mystic Jew like Spinoza or Zangwill is a great and delicate task in which even Dickens might have failed. But most of us know something of the make and manners of the low Jew, who is generally the successful one. Most of us know the Jew who calls himself De Valancourt. Now to any one who knows a low Jew by sight or hearing, the story called *Our Mutual Friend* is literally full of Jews. Like all Dickens's best characters they are vivid; we know them. And we know them to be Hebrew. Mr. Veneering, the Man from Nowhere, dark, sphinx-like, smiling, with black curling hair, and a taste in florid vulgar furniture—of what stock was he? Mr. Lammle, with "too much nose in his face, too much ginger in his whiskers, too much sparkle in his studs and manners"——of what blood was he? Mr. Lammle's friends, coarse and thick-lipped, with fingers so covered with rings that they could hardly hold their gold pencils— do they remind us of anybody? Mr. Fledgeby, with his little ugly eyes and social flashiness and craven bodily servility—might not some fanatic like M. Drumont make interesting conjectures about him? The particular types that people hate in Jewry, the types that are the shame of all good Jews, absolutely run riot in this book, which is supposed to contain an apology to them. It looks at first sight as if Dickens's apology were one hideous sneer. It looks as if he put in one good Jew whom nobody could believe in, and then balanced him with ten bad Jews whom nobody could fail to recognise. It seems as if he had avenged himself for the doubt about Fagin by introducing five or six Fagins—triumphant Fagins, fashionable Fagins, Fagins who had changed their names. The impeccable old Aaron stands up in the middle of this ironic carnival with a peculiar solemnity and silliness. He looks like one particularly stupid Englishman pretending to be a Jew, amidst all that crowd of clever Jews who are pretending to be Englishmen.

But this notion of a sneer is not admissible. Dickens was far too frank and generous a writer to employ such an elaborate plot of silence. His satire was always intended to attack, never to entrap; moreover, he was far too vain a man not to wish the crowd to see all his jokes. Vanity is more divine than pride, because it is more democratic than pride. Third, and most important, Dickens was a good Liberal, and would have been horrified at the notion of making so venomous a vendetta against one race or creed. Nevertheless the fact is there, as I say, if only as a curiosity of literature. I defy any man to read through *Our Mutual Friend* after hearing this suggestion, and to get out of his head the conviction that Lammle is the wrong kind of Jew. The explanation lies, I think, in this, that Dickens was so wonderfully sensitive to that change that has come over our society, that he noticed the type of the oriental and cosmopolitan financier without even knowing that it was oriental or cosmopolitan. He had, in fact, fallen a victim to a very simple fallacy affecting this problem. Somebody said, with great wit and truth, that treason cannot prosper, because when it prospers it cannot be called treason. The same argument soothed all possible Anti-Semitism in men like Dickens. Jews cannot be sneaks and snobs, because when they are sneaks and snobs they do not admit that they are Jews.

I have taken this case of the growth of the cosmopolitan financier, because it is not so stale in discussion as its parallel, the growth of Socialism. But as regards Dickens, the same criticism applies to both. Dickens knew that Socialism was coming, though he did not know its name. Similarly, Dickens knew that the South African millionaire was coming, though he did not know the millionaire's name. Nobody does. His was not a type of mind to disentangle either the abstract truths touching the Socialist, nor the highly personal truth about the millionaire. He was a man of impressions; he has never been equalled in the art of conveying what a man looks like at first sight—and he simply felt the two things as atmospheric facts. He felt that the mercantile power was oppressive, past all bearing by Christian men; and he felt that this power was no longer wholly in the hands even of heavy English merchants like Podsnap. It was largely in the hands of a feverish and unfamiliar type, like Lammle and Veneering. The fact that he felt these things is almost more impressive because he did not understand them.

Now for this reason Dickens must definitely be considered in the light of the changes which his soul foresaw. Thackeray has become classical; but Dickens has done more: he has remained modern. The grand retrospective spirit of Thackeray is by its nature

attached to places and times; he belongs to Queen
Victoria as much as Addison belongs to Queen Anne,
and it is not only Queen Anne who is dead. But Dickens, in a dark prophetic kind of way, belongs to the
developments. He belongs to the times since his
death when Hard Times grew harder, and when
Veneering became not only a Member of Parliament,
but a Cabinet Minister; the times when the very soul
and spirit of Fledgeby carried war into Africa. Dickens
can be criticised as a contemporary of Bernard Shaw or
Anatole France or C. F. G. Masterman. In talking of
him one need no longer talk merely of the Manchester
School or Puseyism or the Charge of the Light Brigade;
his name comes to the tongue when we are talking of
Christian Socialists or Mr. Roosevelt or County Council
Steam Boats or Guilds of Play. He can be considered
under new lights, some larger and some meaner than
his own; and it is a very rough effort so to consider him
which is the excuse of these pages. Of the essays in this
book I desire to say as little as possible; I will discuss
any other subject in preference with a readiness which
reaches to avidity. But I may very curtly apply the
explanation used above to the cases of two or three of
them. Thus in the article on *David Copperfield* I have
done far less than justice to that fine book considered
in its relation to eternal literature; but I have dwelt
at some length upon a particular element in it which
has grown enormous in England after Dickens's death.
Thus again, in introducing the *Sketches by Boz* I have
felt chiefly that I am introducing them to a new generation insufficiently in sympathy with such palpable
and unsophisticated fun. A Board School education,

evolved since Dickens's day, has given to our people a
queer and inadequate sort of refinement, one which
prevents them from enjoying the raw jests of the
Sketches by Boz, but leaves them easily open to that
slight but poisonous sentimentalism which I note amid
all the merits of David Copperfield.   In the same way
I shall speak of *Little Dorrit*, with reference to a school
of pessimistic fiction which did not exist when it was
written, of *Hard Times* in the light of the most modern
crises of economics, and of *The Child's History of England*
in the light of the most matured authority of history.
In short, these criticisms are an intrinsically ephemeral
comment from one generation upon work that will
delight many more.   Dickens was a very great man,
and there are many ways of testing and stating the fact.
But one permissible way is to say this, that he was an
ignorant man, ill-read in the past, and often confused
about the present.   Yet he remains great and true, and
even essentially reliable, if we suppose him to have
known not only all that went before his lifetime, but
also all that was to come after.

From this vanishing of the Victorian compromise
(I might say the Victorian illusion) there begins to
emerge a menacing and even monstrous thing—we
may begin again to behold the English people.   If
that strange dawn ever comes, it will be the final
vindication of Dickens.   It will be proved that he is
hardly even a caricaturist; that he is something very
like a realist.   Those comic monstrosities which the
critics found incredible will be found to be the immense
majority of the citizens of this country.   We shall find
that Sweedlepipe cuts our hair and Pumblechook sells

our cereals; that Sam Weller blacks our boots and Tony Weller drives our omnibus.   For the exaggerated notion of the exaggerations of Dickens (as was admirably pointed out by my old friend and enemy Mr. Blatchford in a *Clarion* review) is very largely due to our mixing with only one social class, whose conventions are very strict, and to whose affectations we are accustomed.   In cabmen, in cobblers, in charwomen, individuality is often pushed to the edge of insanity. But as long as the Thackerayan platform of gentility stood firm all this was, comparatively speaking, concealed.   For the English, of all nations, have the most uniform upper class and the most varied democracy.   In France it is the peasants who are solid to uniformity; it is the marquises who are a little mad. But in England, while good form restrains and levels the universities and the army, the poor people are the most motley and amusing creatures in the world, full of humorous affections and prejudices and twists of irony.   Frenchmen tend to be alike, because they are all soldiers; Prussians because they are all something else, probably policemen; even Americans are all something, though it is not easy to say what it is; it goes with hawk-like eyes and an irrational eagerness.   Perhaps it is savages.   But two English cabmen will be as grotesquely different as Mr. Weller and Mr. Wegg.   Nor is it true to say that I see this variety because it is in my own people.   For I do not see the same degree of variety in my own class or in the class above it; there is more superficial resemblance between two Kensington doctors or two Highland dukes.   No; the democracy is really composed of Dickens characters,

for the simple reason that Dickens was himself one of
the democracy.

There remains one thing to be added to this attempt
to exhibit Dickens in the growing and changing lights
of our time. God forbid that any one (especially any
Dickensian) should dilute or discourage the great efforts
towards social improvement. But I wish that social
reformers would more often remember that they are
imposing their rules not on dots and numbers, but on
Bob Sawyer and Tim Linkinwater, on Mrs. Lirriper
and Dr. Marigold. I wish Mr. Sidney Webb would
shut his eyes until he *sees* Sam Weller.

A great many circumstances have led to the neglect
in literature of these exuberant types which do actually
exist in the ruder classes of society. Perhaps the
principal cause is that since Dickens's time the study
of the poor has ceased to be an art and become a sort
of sham science. Dickens took the poor individually:
all modern writing tends to take them collectively.
It is said that the modern realist produces a photograph
rather than a picture. But this is an inadequate objection. The real trouble with the realist is not that he
produces a photograph, but that he produces a composite photograph. It is like all composite photographs,
blurred; like all composite photographs, hideous; and
like all composite photographs, unlike anything or anybody. The new sociological novels, which attempt to
describe the abstract type of the working-classes, sin
in practice against the first canon of literature, true
when all others are subject to exception. Literature
must always be a pointing out of what is interesting
in life; but these books are duller than the life they

represent. Even supposing that Dickens did **exag-gerate** the degree to which one man differs from another —that was at least an exaggeration upon the side of literature; it was better than a mere attempt to reduce what is actually vivid and unmistakable to what is in comparison colourless or unnoticeable. Even the creditable and necessary efforts of our time in certain matters of social reform have discouraged the old distinctive Dickens treatment. People are so anxious to do something for the poor man that they have a sort of subconscious desire to think that there is only one kind of man to do it for. Thus while the old accounts were sometimes too steep and crazy, the new became too sweeping and flat. People write about the problem of drink, for instance, as if it were one problem. Dickens could have told them that there is the abyss between heaven and hell between the incongruous excesses of Mr. Pickwick and the fatalistic soaking of Mr. Wickfield. He could have shown that there was nothing in common between the brandy and water of Bob Sawyer and the rum and water of Mr. Stiggins. People talk of imprudent marriages among the poor, as if it were all one question. Dickens could have told them that it is one thing to marry without much money, like Stephen Blackpool, and quite another to marry without the smallest intention of ever trying to get any, like Harold Skimpole. People talk about husbands in the working-classes being kind or brutal to their wives, as if that was the one permanent problem and no other possibility need be considered. Dickens could have told them that there was the case (the by no means uncommon case) of the husband of Mrs. Gargery as well as of the wife of Mr. Quilp. In short, Dickens saw the problem of the poor not as a dead and definite business, but as a living and very complex one. In some ways he would be called much more conservative than the modern sociologists, in some ways much more revolutionary.

LITTLE DORRIT

In the time of the decline and death of Dickens, and even more strongly after it, there arose a school of criticism which substantially maintained that a man wrote better when he was ill. It was some such sentiment as this that made Mr. George Gissing, that able writer, come near to contending that *Little Dorrit* is Dickens's best book. It was the principle of his philosophy to maintain (I know not why) that a man was more likely to perceive the truth when in low spirits than when in high spirits.

REPRINTED PIECES

The three articles on Sunday of which I speak are almost the last expression of an articulate sort in English literature of the ancient and existing morality of the English people. It is always asserted that Puritanism came in with the seventeenth century and thoroughly soaked and absorbed the English. We are now, it is constantly said, an incurably Puritanic people. Personally, I have my doubts about this. I shall not refuse to admit to the Puritans that they conquered and crushed the English people; but I do not think that they ever transformed it. My doubt is chiefly derived from three historical facts. First, that England was never so richly and recognisably English as in the Shakespearian age before the Puritan had appeared. Second, that ever since he did appear there has been a long unbroken line of brilliant and typical Englishmen who belonged to the Shakespearian and not the Puritanic tradition; Dryden, Johnson, Wilkes, Fox, Nelson, were hardly Puritans. And third, that the real rise of a new, cold, and illiberal morality in these matters seems to me to have occurred in the time of Queen Victoria, and not of Queen Elizabeth. All things considered, it is likely that future historians will say that the Puritans first really triumphed in the twentieth century, and that Dickens was the last cry of Merry England.

And about these additional, miscellaneous, and even inferior works of Dickens there is, moreover, another use and fascination which all Dickensians will understand; which, after a manner, is not for the profane. All who love Dickens have a strange sense that he is really inexhaustible. It is this fantastic infinity that divides him even from the strongest and healthiest romantic artists of a later day—from Stevenson, for example. I have read *Treasure Island* twenty times; nevertheless I know it. But I do not really feel as if I knew all *Pickwick;* I have not so much read it twenty times as read in it a million times; and it almost seemed as if I always read something new. We of the true faith look at each other and understand; yes, our master was a magician. I believe the books are alive; I believe that leaves still grow in them, as leaves grow on the trees. I believe that this fairy library flourishes and increases like a fairy forest: but the world is listening to us, and we will put our hand upon our mouth.

OUR MUTUAL FRIEND

One thing at least seems certain. Dickens may or may not have been socialist in his tendencies; one might quote on the affirmative side his satire against Mr. Podsnap, who thought Centralisation "un-English"; one might quote in reply the fact that he satirised quite as unmercifully state and municipal officials of the most modern type. But there is one condition of affairs which Dickens would certainly have detested and denounced, and that is the condition in which we actually stand to-day. At this moment it is vain to discuss whether socialism will be a selling of men's liberty for bread. The men have already sold the liberty; only they have not yet got the bread. A most incessant and exacting interference with the poor is already in operation; they are already ruled like slaves, only they are not fed like slaves. The children are forcibly provided with a school; only they are not provided with a house. Officials give the most detailed domestic directions about the fireguard; only they do not give the fireguard. Officials bring round the most stringent directions about the milk; only they do not bring round the milk. The situation is perhaps the most humorous in the whole history of oppression. We force the nigger to dig; but as a concession to him we do not give him a spade. We compel Sambo to cook; but we consult his dignity so far as to refuse him a fire.

This state of things at least cannot conceivably
endure. We must either give the workers more property and liberty, or we must feed them properly as
we work them properly. If we insist on sending the
menu into them, they will naturally send the bill into us.
This may possibly result (it is not my purpose here to
prove that it will) in the drilling of the English people
into hordes of humanely herded serfs; and this again
may mean the fading from our consciousness of all those
elves and giants, monsters and fantastics whom we are
faintly beginning to feel and remember in the land. If
this be so, the work of Dickens may be considered as
a great vision—a vision, as Swinburne said, between
a sleep and a sleep. It can be said that between the
grey past of territorial depression and the grey future
of economic routine the strange clouds lifted, and we
beheld the land of the living.

Lastly, Dickens is even astonishingly right about
Eugene Wrayburne. So far from reproaching him
with not understanding a gentleman, the critic will
be astonished at the accuracy with which he has really
observed the worth and the weakness of the aristocrat.
He is quite right when he suggests that such a man has
intelligence enough to despise the invitations which he
has not the energy to refuse. He is quite right when he
makes Eugene (like Mr. Balfour) constantly right in
argument even when he is obviously wrong in fact.
Dickens is quite right when he describes Eugene as
capable of cultivating a sort of secondary and false
industry about anything that is not profitable; or
pursuing with passion anything that is not his business.
He is quite right in making Eugene honestly apprecia-

tive of essential goodness—in other people. He is quite right in making him really good at the graceful combination of satire and sentiment, both perfectly sincere. He is also right in indicating that the only cure for this intellectual condition is a violent blow on the head.

DAVID COPPERFIELD

The real achievement of the earlier part of *David Copperfield* lies in a certain impression of the little Copperfield living in a land of giants. It is at once Gargantuan in its fancy and grossly vivid in its facts; like Gulliver in the land of Brobdingnag when he describes mountainous hands and faces filling the sky, bristles as big as hedges, or moles as big as molehills. To him parents and guardians are not Olympians (as in Mr. Kenneth Grahame's clever book), mysterious and dignified, dwelling upon a cloudy hill. Rather they are all the more visible for being large. They come all the closer because they are colossal. Their queer features and weaknesses stand out large in a sort of gigantic domesticity, like the hairs and freckles of a Brobdingnagian. We feel the sombre Murdstone coming upon the house like a tall storm striding through the sky. We watch every pucker of Peggotty's peasant face in its moods of flinty prejudice or whimsical hesitation. We look up and feel that Aunt Betsey in her garden gloves was really terrible—especially her garden gloves. But one cannot avoid the impression that as the boy grows larger these figures grow smaller, and are not perhaps so completely satisfactory.

CHRISTMAS BOOKS

And there is doubtless a certain poetic unity and
irony in gathering together three or four of the crudest
and most cocksure of the modern theorists, with their
shrill voices and metallic virtues, under the fulness and
the sonorous sanity of Christian bells. But the figures
satirised in *The Chimes* cross each other's path and spoil
each other in some degree. The main purpose of the
book was a protest against that impudent and hard-
hearted utilitarianism which arranges the people only
in rows of men or even in rows of figures. It is a flaming denunciation of that strange mathematical morality
which was twisted often unfairly out of Bentham and
Mill: a morality by which each citizen must regard
himself as a fraction, and a very vulgar fraction.
Though the particular form of this insolent patronage
has changed, this revolt and rebuke is still of value, and
may be wholesome for those who are teaching the poor
to be provident. Doubtless it is a good idea to be
provident, in the sense that Providence is provident,
but that should mean being kind, and certainly not
merely being cold.

The Cricket on the Hearth, though popular, I think, with
many sections of the great army of Dickensians, cannot be spoken of in any such abstract or serious terms.
It is a brief domestic glimpse; it is an interior. It must
be remembered that Dickens was fond of interiors as
such; he was like a romantic tramp who should go from
window to window looking in at the parlours. He had
that solid, indescribable delight in the mere solidity and
neatness of funny little humanity in its funny little

houses, like doll's houses. To him every house was a box, a Christmas box, in which a dancing human doll was tied up in bricks and slates instead of string and brown paper. He went from one gleaming window to another, looking in at the lamp-lit parlours. Thus he stood for a little while looking in at this cosy if commonplace interior of the carrier and his wife; but he did not stand there very long. He was on his way to quainter towns and villages. Already the plants were sprouting upon the balcony of Miss Tox; and the great wind was rising that flung Mr. Pecksniff against his own front door.

TALE OF TWO CITIES

It was well for him, at any rate, that the people rose in France. It was well for him, at any rate, that the guillotine was set up in the Place de la Concorde. Unconsciously, but not accidentally, Dickens was here working out the whole true comparison between swift revolutionism in Paris and slow evolutionism in London. Sidney Carton is one of those sublime ascetics whose head offends them, and who cut it off. For him at least it was better that the blood should flow in Paris than that the wine should flow any longer in London. And if I say that even now the guillotine might be the best cure for many a London lawyer, I ask you to believe that I am not merely flippant. But you will not believe it.

BARNABY RUDGE

It may be said that there is no comparison between

that explosive opening of the intellect in Paris and
an antiquated madman leading a knot of provincial
Protestants.   The Man of the Hill, says Victor Hugo
somewhere, fights for an idea; the Man of the Forest
for a prejudice.   Nevertheless it remains true that
the enemies of the red cap long attempted to represent
it as a sham decoration in the style of Sim Tappertit.
Long after the revolutionists had shown more than the
qualities of men, it was common among lords and lac-
queys to attribute to them the stagey and piratical
pretentiousness of urchins.   The kings called Napoleon's
pistol a toy pistol even while it was holding up their
coach and mastering their money or their lives; they
called his sword a stage sword even while they ran away
from it.   Something of the same senile inconsistency
can be found in an English and American habit common
until recently: that of painting the South Americans
at once as ruffians wading in carnage, and also as
poltroons playing at war.   They blame them first
for the cruelty of having a fight; and then for the weakness of having a sham fight.   Such, however, since the
French Revolution and before it, has been the fatuous
attitude of certain Anglo-Saxons towards the whole
revolutionary tradition.   Sim Tappertit was a sort of
answer to everything; and the young men were mocked
as 'prentices long after they were masters.   The rising
fortune of the South American republics to-day is
symbolical and even menacing of many things; and it
may be that the romance of riot will not be so much
extinguished as extended; and nearer home we may
have boys being boys again, and in London the cry of
"clubs."

THE UNCOMMERCIAL TRAVELLER

The Uncommercial Traveller is a collection of Dickens's memories rather than of his literary purposes; but it is due to him to say that memory is often more startling in him than prophecy in anybody else. They have the character which belongs to all his vivid incidental writing: that they attach themselves always to some text which is a fact rather than an idea. He was one of those sons of Eve who are fonder of the Tree of Life than of the Tree of Knowledge—even of the knowledge of good and of evil. He was in this profoundest sense a realist. Critics have talked of an artist with his eye on the object. Dickens as an essayist always had his eye on an object before he had the faintest notion of a subject. All these works of his can best be considered as letters; they are notes of personal travel, scribbles in a diary about this or that that really happened. But Dickens was one of the few men who have the two talents that are the whole of literature—and have them both together. First, he could make a thing happen over again; and second, he could make it happen better. He can be called exaggerative; but mere exaggeration conveys nothing of his typical talent. Mere whirlwinds of words, mere melodramas of earth and heaven do not affect us as Dickens affects us, because they are exaggerations of nothing. If asked for an exaggeration of something, their inventors would be entirely dumb. They would not know how to exaggerate a broom-stick; for the life of them they could not exaggerate a tenpenny nail. Dickens always began with the nail or the broom-stick. He always began with a fact even when he was most fanciful; and even when he drew the long bow he was careful to hit the white.

This riotous realism of Dickens has its disadvantage —a disadvantage that comes out more clearly in these casual sketches than in his constructed romances. One grave defect in his greatness is that he was altogether too indifferent to theories.   On large matters he went right by the very largeness of his mind; but in small matters he suffered from the lack of any logical test and ready reckoner.   Hence his comment upon the details of civilisation or reform are sometimes apt to be jerky and jarring, and even grossly inconsistent. So long as a thing was heroic enough to admire, Dickens admired it; whenever it was absurd enough to laugh at he laughed at it: so far he was on sure ground.   But about all the small human projects that lie between the extremes of the sublime and the ridiculous, his criticism was apt to have an accidental quality.   As Matthew Arnold said of the remarks of the Young Man from the Country about the perambulator, they are felt not to be at the heart of the situation.   On a great many occasions the Uncommercial Traveller seems, like other hasty travellers, to be criticising elements and institutions which he has quite inadequately understood; and once or twice the Uncommercial Traveller might almost as well be a Commercial Traveller for all he knows of the countryside.

An instance of what I mean may be found in the amusing article about the nightmares of the nursery. Superficially read it might almost be taken to mean that Dickens disapproved of ghost stories—disapproved of that old and genial horror which nurses can hardly supply fast enough for the children who want it. Dickens, one would have thought, should have been the last man in the world to object to horrible stories, having himself written some of the most horrible that exist in the world. The author of the Madman's Manuscript, of the disease of Monk and the death of Krook, cannot be considered fastidious in the matter of revolting realism or of revolting mysticism. If artistic horror is to be kept from the young, it is at least as necessary to keep little boys from reading *Pickwick* or *Bleak House* as to refrain from telling them the story of Captain Murderer or the terrible tale of Chips. If there was something appalling in the rhyme of Chips and pips and ships, it was nothing compared to that infernal refrain of "Mudstains, bloodstains" which Dickens himself, in one of his highest moments of hellish art, put into *Oliver Twist*.

I take this one instance of the excellent article called "Nurse's Stories" because it is quite typical of all the rest. Dickens (accused of superficiality by those who cannot grasp that there is foam upon deep seas) was really deep about human beings; that is, he was original and creative about them. But about ideas he did tend to be a little superficial. He judged them by whether they hit him, and not by what they were trying to hit. Thus in this book the great wizard of the Christmas ghosts seems almost the enemy of ghost stories; thus the almost melodramatic moralist who created Ralph Nickleby and Jonas Chuzzlewit cannot see the point in original sin; thus the great denouncer of official oppression in England may be found far too indulgent to the basest aspects of the modern police. His theories were less important than his creations, because he was a man of genius. But he himself thought his theories the more important, because he was a man.

SKETCHES BY BOZ

THE greatest mystery about almost any great writer is why he was ever allowed to write at all. The first efforts of eminent men are always imitations; and very often they are bad imitations. The only question is whether the publisher had (as his name would seem to imply) some subconscious connection or sympathy with the public, and thus felt instinctively the presence of something that might ultimately tell; or whether the choice was merely a matter of chance and one Dickens was chosen and another Dickens left. The fact is almost unquestionable: most authors made their reputation by bad books and afterwards supported it by good ones. This is in some degree true even in the case of Dickens. The public continued to call him "Boz" long after the public had forgotten the *Sketches by Boz*. Numberless writers of the time speak of "Boz" as having written *Martin Chuzzlewit* and "Boz" as having written *David Copperfield*. Yet if they had gone back to the original book signed "Boz" they might even have felt that it was vulgar and flippant. This is indeed the chief tragedy of publishers: that they may easily refuse at the same moment the wrong manuscript and the right man. It is easy to see of Dickens now that he was the right man; but a man might have been very well excused if he had not realised

I

that the *Sketches* was the right book. Dickens, I say, is a case for this primary query: whether there was in the first work any clear sign of his higher creative spirit. But Dickens is much less a case for this query than almost all the other great men of his period. The very earliest works of Thackeray are much more unimpressive than those of Dickens. Nay, they are much more vulgar than those of Dickens. And worst of all, they are much more numerous than those of Dickens. Thackeray came much nearer to being the ordinary literary failure than Dickens ever came. Read some of the earliest criticisms of Mr. Yellowplush or Michael Angelo Titmarsh and you will realise that at the very beginning there was more potential clumsiness and silliness in Thackeray than there ever was in Dickens. Nevertheless there was some potential clumsiness and silliness in Dickens; and what there is of it appears here and there in the admirable *Sketches by Boz*.

Perhaps we may put the matter this way: this is the only one of Dickens's works of which it is ordinarily necessary to know the date. To a close and delicate comprehension it is indeed very important that *Nicholas Nickleby* was written at the beginning of Dickens's life, and *Our Mutual Friend* towards the end of it. Nevertheless anybody could understand or enjoy these books, whenever they were written. If *Our Mutual Friend* was written in the Latin of the Dark Ages we should still want it translated. If we thought that *Nicholas Nickleby* would not be written until thirty years hence we should all wait for it eagerly. The general impression produced by Dickens's work is the same as that produced by miraculous visions; it is the destruction of time. Thomas Aquinas said that there was no time in the sight of God; however this may be, there was no time in the sight of Dickens. As a general rule Dickens can be read in any order; not only in any order of books, but even in any order of chapters. In an average Dickens book every part is so amusing and alive that you can read the parts backwards; you can read the quarrel first and then the cause of the quarrel; you can fall in love with a woman in the tenth chapter and then turn back to the first chapter to find out who she is. This is not chaos; it is eternity. It means merely that Dickens instinctively felt all his figures to be immortal souls who existed whether he wrote of them or not, and whether the reader read of them or not. There is a peculiar quality as of celestial pre-existence about the Dickens characters. Not only did they exist before we heard of them, they existed also before Dickens heard of them. As a rule this unchangeable air in Dickens deprives any discussion about date of its point. But as I have said, this is the one Dickens work of which the date *is* essential. It is really an important part of the criticism of this book to say that it is his first book. Certain elements of clumsiness, of obviousness, of evident blunder, actually require the chronological explanation. It is biographically important that this is his first book, almost exactly in the same way that it is biographically important that *The Mystery of Edwin Drood* was his last book. Change or no change, *Edwin Drood* has this plain point of a last story about it: that it is not finished. But if the last book is unfinished, the first book is more unfinished still.

The *Sketches* divide themselves, of course, into two broad classes. One half consists of sketches that are truly and in the strict sense sketches. That is, they are things that have no story and in their outline none of the character of creation; they are merely facts from the street or the tavern or the town hall, noted down as they occurred by an intelligence of quite exceptional vivacity. The second class consists of purely creative things: farces, romances, stories in any case with a non-natural perfection, or a poetical justice, to round them off. One class is admirably represented, for instance, by the sketch describing the Charity Dinner, the other by such a story as that of *Horatio Sparkins*. These things were almost certainly written by Dickens at very various periods of his youth; and early as the harvest is, no doubt it is a harvest and had ripened during a reasonably long time. Nevertheless it is with these two types of narrative that the young Charles Dickens first enters English literature; he enters it with a number of journalistic notes of such things as he has seen happen in streets or offices, and with a number of short stories which err on the side of the extravagant and even the superficial. Journalism had not then, indeed, sunk to the low level which it has since reached. His sketches of dirty London would not have been dirty enough for the modern Imperialist press. Still these first efforts of his are journalism, and sometimes vulgar journalism. It was as a journalist that he attacked the world, as a journalist that he conquered it.

The biographical circumstances will not, of course, be forgotten. The life of Dickens had been a curious one. Brought up in a family just poor enough to be painfully conscious of its prosperity and its respectability, he had been suddenly flung by a financial calamity into a social condition far below his own. For men on that exact edge of the educated class such a transition is really tragic. A duke may become a navvy for a joke, but a clerk cannot become a navvy for a joke. Dickens's parents went to a debtors' prison; Dickens himself went to a far more unpleasant place. The debtors' prison had about it at least that element of amiable compromise and kindly decay which belonged (and belongs still) to all the official institutions of England. But Dickens was doomed to see the very blackest aspect of nineteenth-century England, something far blacker than any mere bad government. He went not to a prison but to a factory. In the musty traditionalism of the Marshalsea old John Dickens could easily remain optimistic. In the ferocious efficiency of the modern factory young Charles Dickens narrowly escaped being a pessimist. He did escape this danger; finally he even escaped the factory itself. His next step in life was, if possible, even more eccentric. He was sent to school; he was sent off like an innocent little boy in Eton collars to learn the rudiments of Latin grammar, without any reference to the fact that he had already taken his part in the horrible competition and actuality of the age of manufactures. It was like giving a sacked bank manager a satchel and sending him to a dame's school. Nor was the third stage of this career unconnected with the oddity of the others. On leaving the school he was made a clerk in a lawyer's office, as if henceforward this child of ridiculous changes was to settle down into a silent assistant for a quiet solicitor. It was exactly at this moment that his fundamental rebellion began to seethe; it seethed more against the quiet finality of his legal occupation than it had seethed against the squalor and slavery of his days of poverty. There must have been in his mind, I think, a dim feeling: "Did all my dark crises mean only this; was I crucified only that I might become a solicitor's clerk?" Whatever be the truth about this conjecture there can be no question about the facts themselves. It was about this time that he began to burst and bubble over, to insist upon his own intellect, to claim a career. It was about this time that he put together a loose pile of papers, satires on institutions, pictures of private persons, fairy tales of the vulgarity of his world, odds and ends such as come out of the facility and the fierce vanity of youth. It was about this time at any rate that he decided to publish them, and gave them the name of *Sketches by Boz*.

They must, I think, be read in the light of this youthful explosion. In some psychological sense he had really been wronged. But he had only become conscious of his wrongs as his wrongs had been gradually righted. Similarly, it has often been found that a man who can patiently endure penal servitude through a judicial blunder will nevertheless, when once his cause is well asserted, quarrel about the amount of compensation or complain of small slights in his professional existence. These are the marks of the first literary action of Dickens. It has in it all the peculiar hardness of youth; a hardness which in those who have in any way been unfairly treated reaches even to impudence. It is a terrible thing for any man to find out that his elders are wrong. And this almost unkindly courage of youth must partly be held responsible for the smartness of Dickens, that almost offensive smartness which in these earlier books of his sometimes irritates us like the showy gibes in the tall talk of a school-boy. These first pages bear witness both to the energy of his genius and also to its unenlightenment; he seems more ignorant and more cocksure than so great a man should be. Dickens was never stupid, but he was sometimes silly; and he is occasionally silly here.

All this must be said to prepare the more fastidious modern for these papers, if he has never read them before. But when all this has been said there remains in them exactly what always remains in Dickens when you have taken away everything that can be taken away by the most fastidious modern who ever dissected his grandmother. There remains that *primum mobile* of which all the mystics have spoken: energy, the power to create. I will not call it "the will to live," for that is a priggish phrase of German professors. Even German professors, I suppose, have the will to live. But Dickens had exactly what German professors have not: he had the power to live. And indeed it is most valuable to have these early specimens of the Dickens work if only because they are specimens of his spirit apart from his matured intelligence. It is well to be able to realise that contact with the Dickens world is almost like a physical contact; it is like stepping suddenly into the hot smells of a greenhouse, or into the bleak smell of the sea. We know that we are there. Let any one read, for instance, one of the foolish but amusing farces in Dickens's first volume. Let him

read, for instance, such a story as that of *Horatio Sparkins*
or that of *The Tuggses at Ramsgate*.   He will not find
very much of that verbal felicity or fantastic irony that
Dickens afterwards developed; the incidents are upon
the plain lines of the stock comedy of the day: sharpers
who entrap simpletons, spinsters who angle for husbands, youths who try to look Byronic and only look
foolish.   Yet there is something in these stories which
there is not in the ordinary stock comedies of that
day: an indefinable flavour of emphasis and richness, a
hint as of infinity of fun.   Doubtless, for instance, a
million comic writers of that epoch had made game of
the dark, romantic young man who pretended to abysses
of philosophy and despair.   And it is not easy to say
exactly why we feel that the few metaphysical remarks
of Mr. Horatio Sparkins are in some way really much
funnier than any of those old stock jokes.   It is in a
certain quality of deep enjoyment in the writer as well
as the reader; as if the few words written had been
dipped in dark nonsense and were, as it were, reeking
with derision.   "Because if Effect be the result of
Cause and Cause be the Precursor of Effect," said Mr.
Horatio Sparkins, "I apprehend that you are wrong."
Nobody can get at the real secret of sentences like that;
sentences which were afterwards strewed with reckless
liberality over the conversation of Dick Swiveller or
Mr. Mantalini, Sim Tappertit or Mr. Pecksniff.
Though the joke seems most superficial one has only
to read it a certain number of times to see that it is
most subtle.   The joke does not lie in Mr. Sparkins
merely using long words, any more than the joke lies
merely in Mr. Swiveller drinking, or in Mr. Mantalini

deceiving his wife. It is something in the arrangement of the words; something in a last inspired turn of absurdity given to a sentence. In spite of everything Horatio Sparkins is funny. We cannot tell why he is funny. When we know why he is funny we shall know why Dickens is great.

Standing as we do here upon the threshold, as it were, of the work of Dickens, it may be well perhaps to state this truth as being, after all, the most important one. This first work had, as I have said, the faults of first work and the special faults that arose from its author's accidental history; he was deprived of education, and therefore it was in some ways uneducated; he was confronted with the folly and failure of his natural superiors and guardians, and therefore it was in some ways pert and insolent. Nevertheless the main fact about the work is worth stating here for any reader who should follow the chronological order and read the *Sketches by Boz* before embarking on the stormy and splendid sea of *Pickwick*. For the sea of *Pickwick*, though splendid, does make some people seasick. The great point to be emphasised at such an initiation is this: that people, especially refined people, are not to judge of Dickens by what they would call the coarseness or commonplaceness of his subject. It is quite true that his jokes are often on the same *subjects* as the jokes in a halfpenny comic paper. Only they happen to be good jokes. He does make jokes about drunkenness, jokes about mothers-in-law, jokes about henpecked husbands, jokes (which is much more really unpardonable) about spinsters, jokes about physical cowardice, jokes about fatness, jokes about sitting down on one's hat.   He does make fun of all these things; and the reason is not very far to seek.   He makes fun of all these things because all these things, or nearly all of them, are really very funny.   But a large number of those who might otherwise read and enjoy Dickens are undoubtedly "put off" (as the phrase goes) by the fact that he seems to be echoing a poor kind of claptrap in his choice of incidents and images.   Partly, of course, he suffers from the very fact of his success; his play with these topics was so good that every one else has played with them increasingly since; he may indeed have copied the old jokes, but he certainly renewed them.   For instance, "Ally Sloper" was certainly copied from Wilkins Micawber.   To this day you may see (in the front page of that fine periodical) the bald head and the high shirt collar that betray the high original from which "Ally Sloper" is derived.   But exactly because "Sloper" was stolen from Micawber, for that very reason the new generation feels as if Micawber were stolen from "Sloper."   Many modern readers feel as if Dickens were copying the comic papers, whereas in truth the comic papers are still copying Dickens.

Dickens showed himself to be an original man by always accepting old and established topics.   There is no clearer sign of the absence of originality among modern poets than their disposition to find new themes. Really original poets write poems about the spring. They are always fresh, just as the spring is always fresh.   Men wholly without originality write poems about torture, or new religions, of some perversion of obscenity, hoping that the mere sting of the subject may speak for them.   But we do not sufficiently realise that what is true of the classic ode is also true of the classic joke. A true poet writes about the spring being beautiful because (after a thousand springs) the spring really is beautiful. In the same way the true humourist writes about a man sitting down on his hat, because the act of sitting down on one's hat (however often and however admirably performed) really is extremely funny. We must not dismiss a new poet because his poem is called *To a Skylark;* nor must we dismiss a humourist because his new farce is called *My Mother-in-law.* He may really have splendid and inspiring things to say upon an eternal problem. The whole question is whether he has.

Now this is exactly where Dickens, and the possible mistake about Dickens, both come in. Numbers of sensitive ladies, numbers of simple æsthetes, have had a vague shrinking from that element in Dickens which begins vaguely in *The Tuggses at Ramsgate* and culminates in *Pickwick.* They have a vague shrinking from the mere subject matter; from the mere fact that so much of the fun is about drinking or fighting, or falling down, or eloping with old ladies. It is to these that the first appeal must be made upon the threshold of Dickens criticism. Let them really read the thing and really see whether the humour is the gross and half-witted jeering which they imagine it to be. It is exactly here that the whole genius of Dickens is concerned. His subjects are indeed stock subjects; like the skylark of Shelley, or the autumn of Keats. But all the more because they are stock subjects the reader realises what a magician is at work. The notion of a clumsy fellow who falls off his horse is indeed a stock

and stale subject.   But Mr. Winkle is not a stock and
stale subject.   Nor is his horse a stock and stale subject;
it is as immortal as the horses of Achilles.   The notion
of a fat old gentleman proud of his legs might easily
be vulgar.   But Mr. Pickwick proud of his legs is not
vulgar; somehow we feel that they were legs to be
proud of.   And it is exactly this that we must look for
in these *Sketches*.   We must not leap to any cheap
fancy that they are low farces.   Rather we must see
that they are not low farces; and see that nobody but
Dickens could have prevented them from being so.

PICKWICK PAPERS

THERE are those who deny with enthusiasm the existence of a God and are happy in a hobby which they call the Mistakes of Moses. I have not studied their labours in detail, but it seems that the chief mistake of Moses was that he neglected to write the Pentateuch. The lesser errors, apparently, were not made by Moses, but by another person equally unknown. These controversialists cover the very widest field, and their attacks upon Scripture are varied to the point of wildness. They range from the proposition that the unexpurgated Bible is almost as unfit for an American girls' school as is an unexpurgated Shakespeare; they descend to the proposition that kissing the Book is almost as hygienically dangerous as kissing the babies of the poor. A superficial critic might well imagine that there was not one single sentence left of the Hebrew or Christian Scriptures which this school had not marked with some ingenious and uneducated comment. But there is one passage at least upon which they have never pounced, at least to my knowledge; and in pointing it out to them I feel that I am, or ought to be, providing material for quite a multitude of Hyde Park orations. I mean that singular arrangement in the mystical account of the Creation by which light is created first and all the luminous bodies afterwards. One could not imagine a process more open to the elephantine logic of the Bible-smasher than this: that the sun should be created after the sunlight. The conception that lies at the back of the phrase is indeed profoundly antagonistic to much of the modern point of view. To many modern people it would sound like saying that foliage existed before the first leaf; it would sound like saying that childhood existed before a baby was born. The idea is, as I have said, alien to most modern thought, and like many other ideas which are alien to most modern thought, it is a very subtle and a very sound idea. Whatever be the meaning of the passage in the actual primeval poem, there is a very real metaphysical meaning in the idea that light existed before the sun and stars. It is not barbaric; it is rather Platonic. The idea existed before any of the machinery which made manifest the idea. Justice existed when there was no need of judges, and mercy existed before any man was oppressed.

However this may be in the matter of religion and philosophy, it can be said with little exaggeration that this truth is the very key of literature. The whole difference between construction and creation is exactly this: that a thing constructed can only be loved after it is constructed; but a thing created is loved before it exists, as the mother can love the unborn child. In creative art the essence of a book exists before the book or before even the details or main features of the book; the author enjoys it and lives in it with a kind of prophetic rapture. He wishes to write a comic

story before he has thought of a single comic incident.
He desires to write a sad story before he has thought of
anything sad. He knows the atmosphere before he
knows anything. There is a low priggish maxim sometimes uttered by men so frivolous as to take humour
seriously—a maxim that a man should not laugh at his
own jokes. But the great artist not only laughs at
his own jokes; he laughs at his own jokes before he has
made them. In the case of a man really humorous
we can see humour in his eye before he has thought
of any amusing words at all. So the creative writer
laughs at his comedy before he creates it, and he has
tears for his tragedy before he knows what it is. When
the symbols and the fulfilling facts do come to him,
they come generally in a manner very fragmentary and
inverted, mostly in irrational glimpses of crisis or con-
summation. The last page comes before the first;
before his romance has begun, he knows that it has
ended well. He sees the wedding before the wooing;
he sees the death before the duel. But most of all
he sees the colour and character of the whole story
prior to any possible events in it. This is the real argument for art and style, only that the artists and the
stylists have not the sense to use it. In one very real
sense style is far more important than either character
or narrative. For a man knows what style of book
he wants to write when he knows nothing else about it.

Pickwick is in Dickens's career the mere mass of
light before the creation of sun or moon. It is the
splendid, shapeless substance of which all his stars were
ultimately made. You might split up *Pickwick* into
innumerable novels as you could split up that primeval

light into innumerable solar systems. The *Pickwick Papers* constitute first and foremost a kind of wild promise, a pre-natal vision of all the children of Dickens. He had not yet settled down into the plain, professional habit of picking out a plot and characters, of attending to one thing at a time, of writing a separate, sensible novel and sending it off to his publishers. He is still in the youthful whirl of the kind of world that he would like to create. He has not yet really settled what story he will write, but only what sort of story he will write. He tries to tell ten stories at once; he pours into the pot all the chaotic fancies and crude experiences of his boyhood; he sticks in irrelevant short stories shamelessly, as into a scrap-book; he adopts designs and abandons them, begins episodes and leaves them unfinished; but from the first page to the last there is a nameless and elemental ecstasy—that of the man who is doing the kind of thing that he can do. Dickens, like every other honest and effective writer, came at last to some degree of care and self-restraint. He learned how to make his *dramatis personæ* assist his drama; he learned how to write stories which were full of rambling and perversity, but which were stories. But before he wrote a single real story, he had a kind of vision. It was a vision of the Dickens world—a maze of white roads, a map full of fantastic towns, thundering coaches, clamorous market-places, uproarious inns, strange and swaggering figures. That vision was *Pickwick*.

It must be remembered that this is true even in connection with the man's contemporaneous biography. Apart from anything else about it, *Pickwick* was his first great chance. It was a big commission given in some sense to an untried man, that he might show what he could do. It was in a strict sense a sample. And just as a sample of leather can be only a piece of leather, or a sample of coal a lump of coal, so this book may most properly be regarded as simply a lump of Dickens. He was anxious to show all that was in him. He was more concerned to prove that he could write well than to prove that he could write this particular book well. And he did prove this, at any rate. No one ever sent such a sample as the sample of Dickens. His roll of leather blocked up the street; his lump of coal set the Thames on fire.

The book originated in the suggestion of a publisher; as many more good books have done than the arrogance of the man of letters is commonly inclined to admit. Very much is said in our time about Apollo and Admetus, and the impossibility of asking genius to work within prescribed limits or assist an alien design. But after all, as a matter of fact, some of the greatest geniuses have done it; from Shakespeare botching up bad comedies and dramatising bad novels down to Dickens writing a masterpiece as the mere framework for a Mr. Seymour's sketches. Nor is the true explanation irrelevant to the spirit and power of Dickens. Very delicate, slender, and *bizarre* talents are indeed incapable of being used for an outside purpose, whether of public good or of private gain. But about very great and rich talent there goes a certain disdainful generosity which can turn its hand to anything. Minor poets cannot write to order; but very great poets can write to order. The larger the man's mind, the wider

his scope of vision, the more likely it will be that anything suggested to him will seem significant and promis-
ing; the more he has a grasp of everything the more
ready he will be to write anything.   It is very hard (if
that is the question) to throw a brick at a man and ask
him to write an epic; but the more he is a great man
the more able he will be to write about the brick.   It
is very unjust (if that is all) to point to a hoarding of
Colman's mustard and demand a flood of philosophical
eloquence; but the greater the man is the more likely
he will be to give it to you.   So it was proved, not for
the first time, in this great experiment of the early
employment of Dickens.   Messrs. Chapman and Hall
came to him with a scheme for a string of sporting
stories to serve as the context, and one might almost
say the excuse, for a string of sketches by Seymour,
the sporting artist.   Dickens made some modifications
in the plan, but he adopted its main feature; and its
main feature was Mr. Winkle.   To think of what Mr.
Winkle might have been in the hands of a dull *farceur*,
and then to think of what he is, is to experience the
feeling that Dickens made a man out of rags and refuse.
Dickens was to work splendidly and successfully in
many fields, and to send forth many brilliant books and
brave figures.   He was destined to have the applause
of [continents like a statesman, and to dictate to his
publishers like a despot; but perhaps he never worked
again so supremely well as here, where he worked in
chains.   It may well be questioned whether his one
hack book is not his masterpiece.

Of course it is true that as he went on his independence increased, and he kicked quite free of the influences

that had suggested his story. So Shakespeare declared his independence of the original chronicle of Hamlet, Prince of Denmark, eliminating altogether (with some wisdom) another uncle called Wiglerus. At the start the Nimrod Club of Chapman and Hall may have even had equal chances with the Pickwick Club of young Mr. Dickens; but the Pickwick Club became something much better than any publisher had dared to dream of. Some of the old links were indeed severed by accident or extraneous trouble; Seymour, for whose sake the whole had perhaps been planned, blew his brains out before he had drawn ten pictures. But such things were trifles compared to *Pickwick* itself. It mattered little now whether Seymour blew his brains out, so long as Charles Dickens blew his brains in. The work became systematically and progressively more powerful and masterly. Many critics have commented on the somewhat discordant and inartistic change between the earlier part of *Pickwick* and the later; they have pointed out, not without good sense, that the character of Mr. Pickwick changes from that of a silly buffoon to that of a solid merchant. But the case, if these critics had noticed it, is much stronger in the minor characters of the great company. Mr. Winkle, who has been an idiot (even, perhaps, as Mr. Pickwick says, "an impostor"), suddenly becomes a romantic and even reckless lover, scaling a forbidden wall and planning a bold elopement. Mr. Snodgrass, who has behaved in a ridiculous manner in all serious positions, suddenly finds himself in a ridiculous position —that of a gentleman surprised in a secret love affair— and behaves in a manner perfectly manly, serious,

and honourable. Mr. Tupman alone has no serious
emotional development, and for this reason it is, pre-
sumably, that we hear less and less of Mr. Tupman
towards the end of the book. Dickens has by this time
got into a thoroughly serious mood—a mood expressed
indeed by extravagant incidents, but none the less
serious for that; and into this Winkle and Snodgrass,
in the character of romantic lovers, could be made to
fit. Mr. Tupman had to be left out of the love affairs;
therefore Mr. Tupman is left out of the book.

Much of the change was due to the entrance of the
greatest character in the story. It may seem strange at
the first glance to say that Sam Weller helped to make
the story serious. Nevertheless, this is strictly true.
The introduction of Sam Weller had, to begin with,
some merely accidental and superficial effects. When
Samuel Weller had appeared, Samuel Pickwick was no
longer the chief farcical character. Weller became the
joker and Pickwick in some sense the butt of his jokes.
Thus it was obvious that the more simple, solemn, and
really respectable this butt could be made the better.
Mr. Pickwick had been the figure capering before the
footlights. But with the advent of Sam, Mr. Pickwick
had become a sort of black background and had to be-
have as such. But this explanation, though true as far
as it goes, is a mean and unsatisfactory one, leaving the
great elements unexplained. For a much deeper and
more righteous reason Sam Weller introduces the more
serious tone of Pickwick. He introduces it because he
introduces something which it was the chief business
of Dickens to preach throughout his life—something
which he never preached so well as when he preached

it unconsciously. Sam Weller introduces the English people.

Sam Weller is the great symbol in English literature of the populace peculiar to England. His incessant stream of sane nonsense is a wonderful achievement of Dickens: but it is no great falsification of the incessant stream of sane nonsense as it really exists among the English poor. The English poor live in an atmosphere of humour; they think in humour. Irony is the very air that they breathe. A joke comes suddenly from time to time into the head of a politician or a gentleman, and then as a rule he makes the most of it; but when a serious word comes into the mind of a coster it is almost as startling as a joke. The word "chaff" was, I suppose, originally applied to badinage to express its barren and unsustaining character; but to the English poor chaff is as sustaining as grain. The phrase that leaps to their lips is the ironical phrase. I remember once being driven in a hansom cab down a street that turned out to be a *cul de sac*, and brought us bang up against a wall. The driver and I simultaneously said something. But I said: "This 'll never do!" and he said: "This is all right!" Even in the act of pulling back his horse's nose from a brick wall, that confirmed satirist thought in terms of his highly-trained and traditional satire; while I, belonging to a duller and simpler class, expressed my feelings in words as innocent and literal as those of a rustic or a child.

This eternal output of divine derision has never been so truly typified as by the character of Sam; he is a grotesque fountain which gushes the living waters

for ever.   Dickens is accused of exaggeration and he
is often guilty of exaggeration; but here he does not
exaggerate: he merely symbolises and sublimates like
any other great artist.   Sam Weller does not exaggerate
the wit of the London street arab one atom more than
Colonel Newcome, let us say, exaggerates the stateliness
of an ordinary soldier and gentleman, or than Mr.
Collins exaggerates the fatuity of a certain kind of
country clergyman.   And this breath from the boister-
ous brotherhood of the poor lent a special seriousness
and smell of reality to the whole story.   The unconscious follies of Winkle and Tupman are blown away
like leaves before the solid and conscious folly of Sam
Weller.   Moreover, the relations between Pickwick and
his servant Sam are in some ways new and valuable
in literature.   Many comic writers had described the
clever rascal and his ridiculous dupe; but here, in a
fresh and very human atmosphere, we have a clever
servant who was not a rascal and a dupe and who was
not ridiculous.   Sam Weller stands in some ways for a
cheerful knowledge of the world; Mr. Pickwick stands
for a still more cheerful ignorance of the world.   And
Dickens responded to a profound human sentiment
(the sentiment that has made saints and the sanctity
of children) when he made the gentler and less-trav-
elled type—the type which moderates and controls.
Knowledge and innocence are both excellent things, and
they are both very funny. But it is right that knowledge
should be the servant and innocence the master.

The sincerity of this study of Sam Weller has produced one particular effect in the book which I wonder

that critics of Dickens have never noticed or discussed. Because it has no Dickens "pathos," certain parts of it are truly pathetic. Dickens, realising rightly that the whole tone of the book was fun, felt that he ought to keep out of it any great experiments in sadness and keep within limits those that he put in. He used this restraint in order not to spoil the humour; but (if he had known himself better) he might well have used it in order not to spoil the pathos. This is the one book in which Dickens was, as it were, forced to trample down his tender feelings; and for that very reason it is the one book where all the tenderness there is is quite unquestionably true. An admirable example of what I mean may be found in the scene in which Sam Weller goes down to see his bereaved father after the death of his step-mother. The most loyal admirer of Dickens can hardly prevent himself from giving a slight shudder when he thinks of what Dickens might have made of that scene in some of his more expansive and maudlin moments. For all I know old Mrs. Weller might have asked what the wild waves were saying; and for all I know old Mr. Weller might have told her. As it is, Dickens, being forced to keep the tale taut and humorous, gives a picture of humble respect and decency which is manly, dignified, and really sad. There is no attempt made by these simple and honest men, the father and son, to pretend that the dead woman was anything greatly other than she was; their respect is for death, and for the human weakness and mystery which it must finally cover. Old Tony Weller does not tell his shrewish wife that she is already a white-winged

angel; he speaks to her with an admirable good nature
and good sense:

"'Susan,' I says, 'you've been a wery good vife to
me altogether: keep a good heart, my dear, and you 'll
live to see me punch that 'ere Stiggins's 'ead yet.' She
smiled at this, Samivel . . . but she died arter all."

That is perhaps the first and the last time that Dickens ever touched the extreme dignity of pathos. He is
restraining his compassion, and afterwards he let it go.
Now laughter is a thing that can be let go; laughter has
in it a quality of liberty. But sorrow has in it by its
very nature a quality of confinement; pathos by its
very nature fights with itself. Humour is expansive;
it bursts outwards; the fact is attested by the common
expression, "holding one's sides." But sorrow is not
expansive; and it was afterwards the mistake of Dickens
that he tried to make it expansive. It is the one great
weakness of Dickens as a great writer, that he did try
to make that sudden sadness, that abrupt pity, which
we call pathos, a thing quite obvious, infectious, public,
as if it were journalism or the measles. It is pleasant to
think that in this supreme masterpiece, done in the
dawn of his career, there is not even this faint fleck upon
the sun of his just splendour. Pickwick will always be
remembered as the great example of everything that
made Dickens great; of the solemn conviviality of great
friendships, of the erratic adventures of old English
roads, of the hospitality of old English inns, of the great
fundamental kindliness and honour of old English
manners. First of all, however, it will always be
remembered for its laughter, or, if you will, for its folly.
A good joke is the one ultimate and sacred thing which

cannot be criticised. Our relations with a good joke are direct and even divine relations. We speak of "seeing" a joke just as we speak of "seeing" a ghost or a vision. If we have seen it, it is futile to argue with us; and we have seen the vision of *Pickwick*. *Pickwick* may be the top of Dickens's humour; I think upon the whole it is. But the broad humour of *Pickwick* he broadened over many wonderful kingdoms; the narrow pathos of *Pickwick* he never found again.

NICHOLAS NICKLEBY

ROMANCE is perhaps the highest point of human expression, except indeed religion, to which it is closely allied. Romance resembles religion especially in this, that it is not only a simplification but a shortening of existence. Both romance and religion see everything as it were foreshortened; they see everything in an abrupt and fantastic perspective, coming to an apex. It is the whole essence of perspective that it comes to a point. Similarly, religion comes to a point—to the point. Thus religion is always insisting on the shortness of human life. But it does not insist on the shortness of human life as the pessimists insist on it. Pessimism insists on the shortness of human life in order to show that life is valueless. Religion insists on the shortness of human life in order to show that life is frightfully valuable—is almost horribly valuable. Pessimism says that life is so short that it gives nobody a chance; religion says that life is so short that it gives everybody his final chance. In the first case the word brevity means futility; in the second case, opportunity. But the case is even stronger than this. Religion shortens everything. Religion shortens even eternity. Where science, submitting to the false standard of time, sees evolution, which is slow, religion sees creation, which is sudden. Philosophically speaking, the process is neither slow nor quick since we have nothing to compare it with. Religion prefers to think of it as quick. For religion the flowers shoot up suddenly like rockets. For religion the mountains are lifted up suddenly like waves. Those who quote that fine passage which says that in God's sight a thousand years are as yesterday that is passed as a watch in the night, do not realise the full force of the meaning. To God a thousand years are not only a watch but an exciting watch. For God time goes at a gallop, as it does to a man reading a good tale.

All this is, in a humble manner, true for romance. Romance is a shortening and sharpening of the human difficulty. Where you and I have to vote against a man, or write (rather feebly) against a man, or sign illegible petitions against a man, romance does for him what we should really like to see done. It knocks him down; it shortens the slow process of historical justice. All romances consist of three characters. Other characters may be introduced; but those other characters are certainly mere scenery as far as the romance is concerned. They are bushes that wave rather excitedly; they are posts that stand up with a certain pride; they are correctly painted rocks that frown very correctly; but they are all landscape—they are all a background. In every pure romance there are three living and moving characters. For the sake of argument they may be called St. George and the Dragon and the Princess. In every romance there must be the twin elements of loving and fighting. In every romance there must be the three characters: there must be the Princess, who is a thing to be loved; there must be the Dragon, who is a thing to be fought; and there must be St. George, who is a thing that both loves and fights. There have been many symptoms of cynicism and decay in our modern civilisation. But of all the signs of modern feebleness, of lack of grasp on morals as they actually must be, there has been none quite so silly or so dangerous as this: that the philosophers of to-day have started to divide loving from fighting and to put them into opposite camps. There could be no worse sign than that a man, even Nietzsche, can be found to say that we should go in for fighting instead of loving. There can be no worse sign than that a man, even Tolstoi, can be found to tell us that we should go in for loving instead of fighting. The two things imply each other; they implied each other in the old romance and in the old religion, which were the two permanent things of humanity. You cannot love a thing without wanting to fight for it. You cannot fight without something to fight for. To love a thing without wishing to fight for it is not love at all; it is lust. It may be an airy, philosophical, and disinterested lust; it may be, so to speak, a virgin lust; but it is lust, because it is wholly self-indulgent and invites no attack. On the other hand, fighting for a thing without loving it is not even fighting; it can only be called a kind of horse-play that is occasionally fatal. Wherever human nature is human and unspoilt by any special sophistry, there exists this natural kinship between war and wooing, and that natural kinship is called romance. It comes upon a man especially in the great hour of youth; and every man who has ever been young at all has felt, if only for a moment, this ultimate and poetic paradox. He knows that loving the world is the same thing as fighting the world. It was at the very moment when he offered to like everybody he also offered to hit everybody. To almost every man that can be called a man this especial moment of the romantic culmination has come. In the first resort the man wished to live a romance. In the second resort, in the last and worst resort, he was content to write one.

Now there is a certain moment when this element enters independently into the life of Dickens. There is a particular time when we can see him suddenly realise that he wants to write a romance and nothing else. In reading his letters, in appreciating his character, this point emerges clearly enough. He was full of the afterglow of his marriage; he was still young and psychologically ignorant; above all, he was now, really for the first time, sure that he was going to be at least some kind of success. There is, I repeat, a certain point at which one feels that Dickens will either begin to write romances or go off on something different altogether. This crucial point in his life is marked by *Nicholas Nickleby*.

It must be remembered that before this issue of *Nicholas Nickleby* his work, successful as it was, had not been such as to dedicate him seriously or irrevocably to the writing of novels. He had already written three books; and at least two of them are classed among the novels under his name. But if we look at the actual origin and formation of these books we see that they came from another source and were really designed upon another plan. The three books were, of course, the *Sketches by Boz*, the *Pickwick Papers*, and *Oliver Twist*.

It is, I suppose, sufficiently well understood that the *Sketches by Boz* are, as their name implies, only sketches. But surely it is quite equally clear that the *Pickwick Papers* are, as their name implies, merely papers. Nor is the case at all different in spirit and essence when we come to *Oliver Twist*. There is indeed a sort of romance in *Oliver Twist*, but it is such an uncommonly bad one that it can hardly be regarded as greatly interrupting the previous process; and if the reader chooses to pay very little attention to it, he cannot pay less attention to it than the author did. But in fact the case lies far deeper. *Oliver Twist* is so much apart from the ordinary track of Dickens, it is so gloomy, it is so much all in one atmosphere, that it can best be considered as an exception or a solitary excursus in his work. Perhaps it can best be considered as the extension of one of his old sketches, of some sketch that happened to be about a visit to a workhouse or a gaol. In the *Sketches by Boz* he might well have visited a workhouse where he saw Bumble; in the *Sketches by Boz* he might well have visited a prison where he saw Fagin. We are still in the realm of sketches and sketchiness. The *Pickwick Papers* may be called an extension of one of his bright sketches. *Oliver Twist* may be called an extension of one of his gloomy ones.

Had he continued along this line all his books might very well have been note-books. It would be very easy to split up all his subsequent books into scraps and episodes, such as those which make up the *Sketches by Boz*. It would be easy enough for Dickens, instead of publishing *Nicholas Nickleby*, to have published a book of sketches, one of which was called "A Yorkshire

School," another called "A Provincial Theatre," and another called "Sir Mulberry Hawk or High Life Revealed," another called " Mrs. Nickleby or a Lady's Monologue." It would have been very easy to have thrown over the rather chaotic plan of the *Old Curiosity Shop*. He might have merely written short stories called "The Glorious Apollos," "Mrs. Quilp's Tea-Party," "Mrs. Jarley's Waxwork," "The Little Servant," and "The Death of a Dwarf." *Martin Chuzzlewit* might have been twenty stories instead of one story. *Dombey and Son* might have been twenty stories instead of one story. We might have lost all Dickens's novels; we might have lost altogether Dickens the novelist. We might have lost that steady love of a seminal and growing romance which grew on him steadily as the years advanced, and which gave us towards the end some of his greatest triumphs. All his books might have been *Sketches by Boz*. But he did turn away from this, and the turning-point is *Nicholas Nickleby*.

Everything has a supreme moment and is crucial; that is where our friends the evolutionists go wrong. I suppose that there is an instant of midsummer as there is an instant of midnight. If in the same way there is a supreme point of spring, *Nicholas Nickleby* is the supreme point of Dickens's spring. I do not mean that it is the best book that he wrote in his youth. *Pickwick* is a better book. I do not mean that it contains more striking characters than any of the other books in his youth. The *Old Curiosity Shop* contains at least two more striking characters. But I mean that this book coincided with his resolution to be a great novelist and his final belief that he could be one.

Henceforward his books are novels, very commonly
bad novels.   Previously they have not really been
novels at all.   There are many indications of the change
I mean.   Here is one, for instance, which is more or
less final.   *Nicholas Nickleby* is Dickens's first romantic
novel because it is his first novel with a proper and
dignified romantic hero; which means, of course, a
somewhat chivalrous young donkey.   The hero of
Pickwick is an old man.   The hero of *Oliver Twist* is a
child.   Even after *Nicholas Nickleby* this non-romantic
custom continued.   The *Old Curiosity Shop* has no
hero in particular.   The hero of *Barnaby Rudge* is a
lunatic.   But Nicholas Nickleby is a proper, formal,
and ceremonial hero.   He has no psychology; he has
not even any particular character; but he is made
deliberately a hero—young, poor, brave, unimpeachable, and ultimately triumphant.   He is, in short, the
hero.   Mr. Vincent Crummles had a colossal intellect;
and I always have a fancy that under all his pomposity
he saw things more keenly than he allowed others to
see.   The moment he saw Nicholas Nickleby, almost
in rags and limping along the high road, he engaged
him (you will remember) as first walking gentleman.
He was right.   Nobody could possibly be more of a
first walking gentleman than Nicholas Nickleby was.
He was the first walking gentleman before he went on
to the boards of Mr. Vincent Crummles's theatre, and
he remained the first walking gentleman after he had
come off.

Now this romantic method involves a certain element
of climax which to us appears crudity.   Nicholas
Nickleby, for instance, wanders through the world; he

takes a situation as assistant to a Yorkshire schoolmaster; he sees an act of tyranny of which he strongly
disapproves; he cries out "Stop!" in a voice that makes
the rafters ring; he thrashes the schoolmaster within
an inch of his life; he throws the schoolmaster away
like an old cigar, and he goes away. The modern
intellect is positively prostrated and flattened by this
rapid and romantic way of righting wrongs. If a
modern philanthropist came to Dotheboys Hall I fear
he would not employ the simple, sacred, and truly
Christian solution of beating Mr. Squeers with a stick.
I fancy he would petition the Government to appoint
a Royal Commission to inquire into Mr. Squeers. I
think he would every now and then write letters to
newspapers reminding people that, in spite of all
appearances to the contrary, there was a Royal Commission to inquire into Mr. Squeers. I agree that he
might even go the length of calling a crowded meeting
in St. James's Hall on the subject of the best policy
with regard to Mr. Squeers. At this meeting some very
heated and daring speakers might even go the length of
alluding sternly to Mr. Squeers. Occasionally even
hoarse voices from the back of the hall might ask (in
vain) what was going to be done with Mr. Squeers.
The Royal Commission would report about three years
afterwards and would say that many things had happened which were certainly most regrettable; that
Mr. Squeers was the victim of a bad system; that Mrs.
Squeers was also the victim of a bad system; but that
the man who sold Squeers his cane had really acted
with great indiscretion and ought to be spoken to
kindly. Something like this would be what, after four

years, the Royal Commission would have said; but
it would not matter in the least what the Royal Commission had said, for by that time the philanthropists
would be off on a new tack and the world would have
forgotten all about Dotheboys Hall and everything
connected with it. By that time the philanthropists
would be petitioning Parliament for another Royal
'Commission; perhaps a Royal Commission to inquire
into whether Mr. Mantalini was extravagant with his
wife's money; perhaps a commission to inquire into
whether Mr. Vincent Crummles kept the Infant Phenomenon short by means of gin.

If we wish to understand the spirit and the period of
Nicholas Nickleby we must endeavour to comprehend
and to appreciate the old more decisive remedies, or,
if we prefer to put it so, the old more desperate remedies.
Our fathers had a plain sort of pity; if you will, a gross
and coarse pity. They had their own sort of sentimentalism. They were quite willing to weep over Smike.
But it certainly never occurred to them to weep over
Squeers. Even those who opposed the French war
opposed it exactly in the same way as their enemies
opposed the French soldiers. They fought with fighting. Charles Fox was full of horror at the bitterness
and the useless bloodshed; but if any one had insulted
him over the matter, he would have gone out and shot
him in a duel as coolly as any of his contemporaries.
All their interference was heroic interference. All
their legislation was heroic legislation. All their
remedies were heroic remedies. No doubt they were
often narrow and often visionary. No doubt they often
looked at a political formula when they should have

looked at an elemental fact. No doubt they were
pedantic in some of their principles and clumsy in some
of their solutions. No doubt, in short, they were all
very wrong; and no doubt we are the people, and wisdom shall die with us. But when they saw something
which in their eyes, such as they were, really violated
their morality, such as it was, then they did not cry
"Investigate!" They did not cry "Educate!" They
did not cry "Improve!" They did not cry "Evolve!"
Like Nicholas Nickleby they cried "Stop!" And it
did stop.

This is the first mark of the purely romantic method:
the swiftness and simplicity with which St. George
kills the dragon. The second mark of it is exhibited
here as one of the weaknesses of *Nicholas Nickleby*. I
mean the tendency in the purely romantic story to
regard the heroine merely as something to be won; to
regard the princess solely as something to be saved from
the dragon. The father of Madeline Bray is really a
very respectable dragon. His selfishness is suggested
with much more psychological tact and truth than that
of any other of the villains that Dickens described
about this time. But his daughter is merely the young
woman with whom Nicholas is in love. We do not
care a rap about Madeline Bray. Personally I should
have preferred Cecilia Bobster. Here is one real point
where the Victorian romance falls below the Elizabethan romantic drama. Shakespeare always made
his heroines heroic as well as his heroes.

In Dickens's actual literary career it is this romantic
quality in *Nicholas Nickleby* that is most important.
It is his first definite attempt to write a young and chiv-

alrous novel.   In this sense the comic characters and the comic scenes are secondary; and indeed the comic characters and the comic scenes, admirable as they are, could never be considered as in themselves superior to such characters and such scenes in many of the other books.   But in themselves how unforgettable they are. Mr. Crummles and the whole of his theatrical business is an admirable case of that first and most splendid quality in Dickens—I mean the art of making something which in life we call pompous and dull, becoming in literature pompous and delightful.   I have remarked before that nearly every one of the amusing characters of Dickens is in reality a great fool.   But I might go further.   Almost every one of his amusing characters is in reality a great bore.   The very people that we fly to in Dickens are the very people that we fly from in life.   And there is more in Crummles than the mere entertainment of his solemnity and his tedium.   The enormous seriousness with which he takes his art is always an exact touch in regard to the unsuccessful artist.   If an artist is successful, everything then depends upon a dilemma of his moral character.   If he is a mean artist success will make him a society man. If he is a magnanimous artist, success will make him an ordinary man.   But only as long as he is unsuccessful will he be an unfathomable and serious artist, like Mr. Crummles.   Dickens was always particularly good at expressing thus the treasures that belong to those who do not succeed in this world.   There are vast prospects and splendid songs in the point of view of the typically unsuccessful man; if all the used-up actors and spoilt journalists and broken clerks could give a chorus, it would be a wonderful chorus in praise of the world. But these unsuccessful men commonly cannot even speak.   Dickens is the voice of them, and a very ringing voice; because he was perhaps the only one of these unsuccessful men that was ever successful.

OLIVER TWIST

In considering Dickens, as we almost always must consider him, as a man of rich originality, we may possibly miss the forces from which he drew even his original energy. It is not well for man to be alone. We, in the modern world, are ready enough to admit that when it is applied to some problem of monasticism or of an ecstatic life. But we will not admit that our modern artistic claim to absolute originality is really a claim to absolute unsociability; a claim to absolute loneliness. The anarchist is at least as solitary as the ascetic. And the men of very vivid vigour in literature, the men such as Dickens, have generally displayed a large sociability towards the society of letters, always expressed in the happy pursuit of pre-existent themes, sometimes expressed, as in the case of Molière or Sterne, in downright plagiarism. For even theft is a confession of our dependence on society. In Dickens, however, this element of the original foundations on which he worked is quite especially difficult to determine. This is partly due to the fact that for the present reading public he is practically the only one of his long line that is read at all. He sums up Smollett and Goldsmith, but he also destroys them. This one giant, being closest to us, cuts off from our view even the giants that begat him. But much more is this difficulty due to the fact that Dickens mixed up with the old material, materials so subtly modern, so made of the French Revolution, that the whole is transformed. If we want the best example of this, the best example is *Oliver Twist*.

Relatively to the other works of Dickens *Oliver Twist* is not of great value, but it is of great import- ance. Some parts of it are so crude and of so clumsy a melodrama, that one is almost tempted to say that Dickens would have been greater without it. But even if he had been greater without it he would still have been incomplete without it. With the exception of some gorgeous passages, both of humour and horror, the interest of the book lies not so much in its revelation of Dickens's literary genius as in its revelation of those moral, personal, and political instincts which were the make-up of his character and the permanent support of that literary genius. It is by far the most depressing of all his books; it is in some ways the most irritating; yet its ugliness gives the last touch of honesty to all that spontaneous and splendid output. Without this one discordant note all his merriment might have seemed like levity.

Dickens had just appeared upon the stage and set the whole world laughing with his first great story *Pickwick*. *Oliver Twist* was his encore. It was the second opportunity given to him by those who had rolled about with laughter over Tupman and Jingle, Weller and Dowler. Under such circumstances a stagey reciter will sometimes take care to give a pathetic piece after his humorous one; and with all his many moral merits, there was much that was stagey about Dickens. But this explanation alone is altogether inadequate and unworthy. There was in Dickens this other kind of energy, horrible, uncanny, barbaric, capable in another age of coarseness, greedy for the emblems of established ugliness, the coffin, the gibbet, the bones, the bloody knife. Dickens liked these things and he was all the more of a man for liking them; especially he was all the more of a boy. We can all recall with pleasure the fact that Miss Petowker (afterwards Mrs. Lillyvick) was in the habit of reciting a poem called "The Blood Drinker's Burial." I cannot express my regret that the words of this poem are not given; for Dickens would have been quite as capable of writing "The Blood Drinker's Burial" as Miss Petowker was of reciting it. This strain existed in Dickens alongside of his happy laughter; both were allied to the same robust romance. Here as elsewhere Dickens is close to all the permanent human things. He is close to religion, which has never allowed the thousand devils on its churches to stop the dancing of its bells. He is allied to the people, to the real poor, who love nothing so much as to take a cheerful glass and to talk about funerals. The extremes of his gloom and gaiety are the mark of religion and democracy; they mark him off from the moderate happiness of philosophers, and from that stoicism which is the virtue and the creed of aristocrats. There is nothing odd in the fact that the same man who conceived the humane hospitalities of Pickwick should also have imagined the inhuman laughter of Fagin's den. They are both genuine and they are both exaggerated. And the whole human tradition has tied up together in a strange knot these strands of festivity and fear. It is over the cups of Christmas Eve that men have always competed in telling ghost stories.

This first element was present in Dickens, and it is very powerfully present in *Oliver Twist*. It had not been present with sufficient consistency or continuity in *Pickwick* to make it remain on the reader's memory at all, for the tale of "Gabriel Grubb" is grotesque rather than horrible, and the two gloomy stories of the "Madman" and the "Queer Client" are so utterly irrelevant to the tale, that even if the reader remember them he probably does not remember that they occur in *Pickwick*. Critics have complained of Shakespeare and others for putting comic episodes into a tragedy. It required a man with the courage and coarseness of Dickens actually to put tragic episodes into a farce. But they are not caught up into the story at all. In *Oliver Twist*, however, the thing broke out with an almost brutal inspiration, and those who had fallen in love with Dickens for his generous buffoonery may very likely have been startled at receiving such very different fare at the next helping. When you have bought a man's book because you like his writing about Mr. Wardle's punch-bowl and Mr. Winkle's skates, it may very well be surprising to open it and read about the sickening thuds that beat out the life of Nancy, or that mysterious villain whose face was blasted with disease.

As a nightmare, the work is really admirable. Characters which are not very clearly conceived as regards their own psychology are yet, at certain moments, managed so as to shake to its foundations our own psychology. Bill Sikes is not exactly a real man, but for all that he is a real murderer. Nancy is not really impressive as a living woman; but (as the phrase goes) she makes a lovely corpse. Something quite childish and eternal in us, something which is shocked with the mere simplicity of death, quivers when we read of those repeated blows or see Sikes cursing the tell-tale cur who will follow his bloody foot-prints. And this strange, sublime, vulgar melodrama, which is melodrama and yet is painfully real, reaches its hideous height in that fine scene of the death of Sikes, the besieged house, the boy screaming within, the crowd screaming without, the murderer turned almost a maniac and dragging his victim uselessly up and down the room, the escape over the roof, the rope swiftly running taut, and death sudden, startling and symbolic; a man hanged. There is in this and similar scenes something of the quality of Hogarth and many other English moralists of the early eighteenth century. It is not easy to define this Hogarthian quality in words, beyond saying that it is a sort of alphabetical realism, like the cruel candour of children. But it has about it these two special principles which separate it from all that we call realism in our time. First, that with us a moral story means a story about moral people; with them a moral story meant more often a story about immoral people. Second, that with us realism is always associated with some subtle view of morals; with them realism was always associated with some simple view of morals. The end of Bill Sikes exactly in the way that the law would have killed him—this is a Hogarthian incident; it carries on that tradition of startling and shocking platitude.

All this element in the book was a sincere thing in the author, but none the less it came from old soils, from the graveyard and the gallows, and the lane where the ghost walked. Dickens was always attracted to such things, and (as Forster says with inimitable simplicity) "but for his strong sense might have fallen into the follies of spiritualism." As a matter of fact, like most of the men of strong sense in his tradition, Dickens was left with a half belief in spirits which became in practice a belief in bad spirits. The great disadvantage of those who have too much strong sense to believe in supernaturalism is that they keep last the low and little forms of the supernatural, such as omens, curses, spectres, and retributions, but find a high and happy supernaturalism quite incredible. Thus the Puritans denied the sacraments, but went on burning witches. This shadow does rest, to some extent, upon the rational English writers like Dickens; supernaturalism was dying, but its ugliest roots died last. Dickens would have found it easier to believe in a ghost than in a vision of the Virgin with angels. There, for good or evil, however, was the root of the old *diablerie* in Dickens, and there it is in *Oliver Twist*. But this was only the first of the new Dickens elements, which must have surprised those Dickensians who eagerly bought his second book. The second of the new Dickens elements is equally indisputable and separate. It swelled afterwards to enormous proportions in Dickens's work; but it really has its rise here. Again, as in the case of the element of *diablerie*, it would be possible to make technical exceptions in favour of *Pickwick*. Just as there were quite inappropriate scraps of the gruesome element in *Pickwick*, so there are quite inappropriate allusions to this other topic in *Pickwick*. But nobody by merely reading *Pickwick* would even remember this topic; no one by merely reading *Pickwick* would know what this topic is; this third great subject of Dickens; this second great subject of the Dickens of *Oliver Twist*.

This subject is social oppression. It is surely fair to say that no one could have gathered from *Pickwick* how this question boiled in the blood of the author of *Pickwick*. There are, indeed, passages, particularly in connection with Mr. Pickwick in the debtor's prison, which prove to us, looking back on a whole public career, that Dickens had been from the beginning bitter and inquisitive about the problem of our civilisation. No one could have imagined at the time that this bitterness ran in an unbroken river under all the surges of that superb gaiety and exuberance. With *Oliver Twist* this sterner side of Dickens was suddenly revealed. For the very first pages of *Oliver Twist* are stern even when they are funny. They amuse, but they cannot be enjoyed, as can the passages about the follies of Mr. Snodgrass or the humiliations of Mr. Winkle. The difference between the old easy humour and this new harsh humour is a difference not of degree but of kind. Dickens makes game of Mr. Bumble because he wants to kill Mr. Bumble; he made game of Mr. Winkle because he wanted him to live for ever. Dickens has taken the sword in hand; against what is he declaring war?

It is just here that the greatness of Dickens comes in; it is just here that the difference lies between the pedant and the poet. Dickens enters the social and political war, and the first stroke he deals is not only significant but even startling. Fully to see this we must appreciate the national situation. It was an age of reform, and even of radical reform; the world was full of radicals and reformers; but only too many of them took the line of attacking everything and anything that was opposed to some particular theory among the many political theories that possessed the end of the eighteenth century. Some had so much perfected the perfect theory of republicanism that they almost lay awake at night because Queen Victoria had a crown on her head. Others were so certain that mankind had hitherto been merely strangled in the bonds of the State that they saw truth only in the destruction of tariffs or of by-laws. The greater part of that generation held that clearness, economy, and a hard common-sense, would soon destroy the errors that had been erected by the superstitions and sentimentalities of the past. In pursuance of this idea many of the new men of the new century, quite confident that they were invigorating the new age, sought to destroy the old sentimental clericalism, the old sentimental feudalism, the old-world belief in priests, the old-world belief in patrons, and among other things the old-world belief in beggars. They sought among other things to clear away the old visionary kindliness on the subject of vagrants. Hence those reformers enacted not only a new reform bill but also a new poor law. In creating many other modern things they created the modern workhouse, and when Dickens came out to fight it was the first thing that he broke with his battle-axe.

This is where Dickens's social revolt is of more value than mere politics and avoids the vulgarity of the novel with a purpose. His revolt is not a revolt of the commercialist against the feudalist, of the Nonconformist against the Churchman, of the Free-trader against the Protectionist, of the Liberal against the Tory. If he were among us now his revolt would not be the revolt of the Socialist against the Individualist, or of the Anarchist against the Socialist. His revolt was simply and solely the eternal revolt; it was the revolt of the weak against the strong. He did not dislike this or that argument for oppression; he disliked oppression. He disliked a certain look on the face of a man when he looks down on another man. And that look on the face is, indeed, the only thing in the world that we have really to fight between here and the fires of Hell. That which pedants of that time and this time would have called the sentimentalism of Dickens was really simply the detached sanity of Dickens. He cared nothing for the fugitive explanations of the Constitutional Conservatives; he cared nothing for the fugitive explanations of the Manchester School. He would have cared quite as little for the fugitive explanations of the Fabian Society or of the modern scientific Socialist. He saw that under many forms there was one fact, the tyranny of man over man; and he struck at it when he saw it, whether it was old or new. When he found that footmen and rustics were too much afraid of Sir Leicester Dedlock, he attacked Sir Leicester Dedlock; he did not care whether Sir Leicester Dedlock said he was attacking England or whether Mr. Rouncewell, the Ironmaster, said he was attacking an effete oligarchy. In that case he pleased Mr. Rouncewell, the Ironmaster, and displeased Sir Leicester Dedlock, the Aristocrat. But when he found that Mr. Rouncewell's workmen were much too frightened of Mr. Rouncewell, then he displeased Mr. Rouncewell in turn; he displeased Mr. Rouncewell very much by calling him Mr. Bounderby. When he imagined himself to be fighting old laws he gave a sort of vague and general approval to new laws. But when he came to the new laws they had a bad time. When Dickens found that after a hundred economic arguments and granting a hundred economic considerations, the fact remained that paupers in modern workhouses were much too afraid of the beadle, just as vassals in ancient castles were much too afraid of the Dedlocks, then he struck suddenly and at once. This is what makes the opening chapters of *Oliver Twist* so curious and important. The very fact of Dickens's distance from, and independence of, the elaborate financial arguments of his time, makes more definite and dazzling his sudden assertion that he sees the old human tyranny in front of him as plain as the sun at noon-day. Dickens attacks the modern workhouse with a sort of inspired simplicity as of a boy in a fairy tale who had wandered about, sword in hand, looking for ogres and who had found an indisputable ogre. All the other people of his time are attacking things because they are bad economics or because they are bad politics, or because they are bad science; he alone is attacking things because they are bad. All the others are Radicals with a large R; he

alone is radical with a small one. He encounters evil
with that beautiful surprise which, as it is the beginning
of all real pleasure, is also the beginning of all righteous
indignation. He enters the workhouse just as Oliver
Twist enters it, as a little child.

This is the real power and pathos of that celebrated
passage in the book which has passed into a proverb;
but which has not lost its terrible humour even in being
hackneyed. I mean, of course, the everlasting quotation about Oliver Twist asking for more. The real
poignancy that there is in this idea is a very good study
in that strong school of social criticism which Dickens
represented. A modern realist describing the dreary
workhouse would have made all the children utterly
crushed, not daring to speak at all, not expecting anything, not hoping anything, past all possibility of
affording even an ironical contrast or a protest of despair. A modern, in short, would have made all the
boys in the workhouse pathetic by making them all
pessimists. But Oliver Twist is not pathetic because
he is a pessimist. Oliver Twist is pathetic because he is
an optimist. The whole tragedy of that incident is in
the fact that he does expect the universe to be kind to
him, that he does believe that he is living in a just
world. He comes before the Guardians as the ragged
peasants of the French Revolution came before the
Kings and Parliaments of Europe. That is to say,
he comes, indeed, with gloomy experiences, but he
comes with a happy philosophy. He knows that there
are wrongs of man to be reviled; but he believes also
that there are rights of man to be demanded. It has
often been remarked as a singular fact that the French

poor, who stand in historic tradition as typical of all the desperate men who have dragged down tyranny, were, as a matter of fact, by no means worse off than the poor of many other European countries before the Revolution. The truth is that the French were tragic because they were better off. The others had known the sorrowful experiences; but they alone had known the splendid expectation and the original claims. It was just here that Dickens was so true a child of them and of that happy theory so bitterly applied. They were the one oppressed people that simply asked for justice; they were the one Parish Boy who innocently asked for more.

OLD CURIOSITY SHOP

NOTHING is important except the fate of the soul; and literature is only redeemed from an utter triviality, surpassing that of naughts and crosses, by the fact that it describes not the world around us or the things on the retina of the eye or the enormous irrelevancy of encyclopædias, but some condition to which the human spirit can come. All good writers express the state of their souls, even (as occurs in some cases of very good writers) if it is a state of damnation. The first thing that has to be realised about Dickens is this ultimate spiritual condition of the man, which lay behind all his creations. This Dickens state of mind is difficult to pick out in words as are all elementary states of mind; they cannot be described, not because they are too subtle for words, but because they are too simple for words. Perhaps the nearest approach to a statement of it would be this: that Dickens expresses an eager anticipation of everything that will happen in the motley affairs of men; he looks at the quiet crowd waiting for it to be picturesque and to play the fool; he expects everything; he is torn with a happy hunger. Thackeray is always looking back to yesterday; Dickens is always looking forward to to-morrow. Both are profoundly humorous, for there is a humour of the morning and a humour of the evening; but the first

guesses at what it will get, at all the grotesqueness and
variety which a day may bring forth; the second looks
back on what the day has been and sees even its solem-
nities as slightly ironical. Nothing can be too extravagant for the laughter that looks forward; and nothing
can be too dignified for the laughter that looks back.
It is an idle but obvious thing, which many must have
noticed, that we often find in the title of one of an
author's books what might very well stand for a general
description of all of them. Thus all Spenser's works
might be called *A Hymn to Heavenly Beauty;* or all
Mr. Bernard Shaw's bound books might be called *You
Never Can Tell.* In the same way the whole substance
and spirit of Thackeray might be gathered under the
general title *Vanity Fair.* In the same way too the
whole substance and spirit of Dickens might be gathered
under the general title *Great Expectations.*

In a recent criticism on this position I saw it
remarked that all this is reading into Dickens something that he did not mean; and I have been told that
it would have greatly surprised Dickens to be informed
that he "went down the broad road of the Revolution." Of course it would. Criticism does not exist
to say about authors the things that they knew themselves. It exists to say the things about them which
they did not know themselves. If a critic says that the
Iliad has a pagan rather than a Christian pity, or that
it is full of pictures made by one epithet, of course he
does not mean that Homer could have said that. If
Homer could have said that the critic would leave
Homer to say it. The function of criticism, if it has a
legitimate function at all, can only be one function—

that of dealing with the subconscious part of the author's mind which only the critic can express, and not with the conscious part of the author's mind, which the author himself can express. Either criticism is no good at all (a very defensible position) or else criticism means saying about an author the very things that would have made him jump out of his boots.

Doubtless the name in this case *Great Expectations* is an empty coincidence; and indeed it is not in the books of the later Dickens period (the period of *Great Expectations*) that we should look for the best examples of this sanguine and expectant spirit which is the essential of the man's genius. There are plenty of good examples of it especially in the earlier works. But even in the earlier works there is no example of it more striking or more satisfactory than *The Old Curiosity Shop*. It is particularly noticeable in the fact that its opening and original framework express the idea of a random experience, a thing come across in the street; a single face in the crowd, followed until it tells its story. Though the thing ends in a novel it begins in a sketch; it begins as one of the *Sketches by Boz*. There is something unconsciously artistic in the very clumsiness of this opening. Master Humphrey starts to keep a scrap-book of all his adventures, and he finds that he can fill the whole scrap-book with the sequels and developments of one adventure; he goes out to notice everybody and he finds himself busily and variedly occupied only in watching somebody. In this there is a very profound truth about the true excitement and inexhaustible poetry of life. The truth is not so much that eternity is full of souls as that one soul can fill eternity. In strict art there is something quite lame and lumbering about the way in which the benevolent old story-teller starts to tell many stories and then drops away altogether, while one of his stories takes his place. But in a larger art, his collision with Little Nell and his complete eclipse by her personality and narrative have a real significance. They suggest the random richness of such meetings, and their uncalculated results. It makes the whole book a sort of splendid accident.

It is not true, as is commonly said, that the Dickens pathos as pathos is bad. It is not true, as is still more commonly said, that the whole business about Little Nell is bad. The case is more complex than that. Yet complex as it is it admits of one sufficiently clear distinction. Those who have written about the death of Little Nell, have generally noticed the crudities of the character itself; the little girl's unnatural and staring innocence, her constrained and awkward piety. But they have nearly all of them entirely failed to notice that there is in the death of Little Nell one quite definite and really artistic idea. It is not an artistic idea that a little child should die rhetorically on the stage like Paul Dombey; and Little Nell does not die rhetorically upon the stage like Paul Dombey. But it is an artistic idea that all the good powers and personalities in the story should set out in pursuit of one insignificant child, to repair an injustice to her, should track her from town to town over England with all the resources of wealth, intelligence, and travel, and should all—arrive too late. All the good fairies and all the kind magicians, all the just kings and all the gallant princes, with chariots and flying dragons and armies and navies go after one little child who had strayed into a wood, and find her dead. That is the conception which Dickens's artistic instinct was really aiming at when he finally condemned Little Nell to death, after keeping her, so to speak, so long with the rope round her neck. The death of Little Nell is open certainly to the particular denial which its enemies make about it. The death of Little Nell is not pathetic. It is perhaps tragic; it is in reality ironic. Here is a very good case of the injustice to Dickens on his purely literary side. It is not that I say that Dickens achieved what he designed; it is that the critics will not see what the design was. They go on talking of the death of Little Nell as if it were a mere example of maudlin description like the death of Little Paul. As a fact it is not described at all; so it cannot be objectionable. It is not the death of Little Nell, but the life of Little Nell, that I object to.

In this, in the actual picture of her personality, if you can call it a personality, Dickens did fall into some of his facile vices. The real objection to much of his pathos belongs really to another part of his character. It is connected with his vanity, his voracity for all kinds of praise, his restive experimentalism and even perhaps his envy. He strained himself to achieve pathos. His humour was inspiration; but his pathos was ambition. His laughter was lonely; he would have laughed on a desert island. But his grief was gregarious. He liked to move great masses of men, to melt them into tenderness, to play on the people as a great pianist plays on them; to make them mad or sad. His pathos was to him a way of showing his power; and for that reason it was really powerless. He could not help making people laugh; but he tried to make them cry. We come in this novel, as we often do come in his novels, upon hard lumps of unreality, upon a phrase that suddenly sickens. That is always due to his conscious despotism over the delicate feelings; that is always due to his love of fame as distinct from his love of fun. But it is not true that all Dickens's pathos is like this; it is not even true that all the passages about Little Nell are like this; there are two strands almost everywhere and they can be differentiated as the sincere and the deliberate. There is a great difference between Dickens thinking about the tears of his characters and Dickens thinking about the tears of his audience.

When all this is allowed, however, and the exaggerated contempt for the Dickens pathos is properly corrected, the broad fact remains: that to pass from the solemn characters in this book to the comic characters in this book, is to be like some Ulysses who should pass suddenly from the land of shadows to the mountain of the gods. Little Nell has her own position in careful and reasonable criticism: even that wobbling old ass, her grandfather, has his position in it; perhaps even the dissipated Fred (whom long acquaintance with Mr. Dick Swiveller has not made any less dismal in his dissipation) has a place in it also. But when we come to Swiveller and Sampson Brass and Quilp and Mrs. Jarley, then Fred and Nell and the grandfather simply do not exist. There are no such people in the story. The real hero and heroine of *The Old Curiosity Shop* are of course Dick Swiveller and the Marchioness.

It is significant in a sense that these two sane, strong, living, and lovable human beings are the only two, or almost the only two, people in the story who do not run after Little Nell. They have something better to do than to go on that shadowy chase after that cheerless phantom. They have to build up between them a true romance; perhaps the one true romance in the whole of Dickens. Dick Swiveller really has all the half-heroic characteristics which make a man respected by a woman and which are the male contribution to virtue. He is brave, magnanimous, sincere about himself, amusing, absurdly hopeful; above all, he is both strong and weak. On the other hand the Marchioness really has all the characteristics, the entirely heroic characteristics which make a woman respected by a man. She is female: that is, she is at once incurably candid and incurably loyal, she is full of terrible common-sense, she expects little pleasure for herself and yet she can enjoy bursts of it; above all, she is physically timid and yet she can face anything. All this solid rocky romanticism is really implied in the speech and action of these two characters and can be felt behind them all the time. Because they are the two most absurd people in the book they are also the most vivid, human, and imaginable. There are two really fine love affairs in Dickens; and I almost think only two. One is the happy courtship of Swiveller and the Marchioness; the other is the tragic courtship of Toots and Florence Dombey. When Dick Swiveller wakes up in bed and sees the Marchioness playing cribbage he thinks that he and she are a prince and princess in a fairy tale. He thinks right.

I speak thus seriously of such characters with a deliberate purpose; for the frivolous characters of Dickens are taken much too frivolously. It has been quite insufficiently pointed out that all the serious moral ideas that Dickens did contrive to express he expressed altogether through this fantastic medium, in such figures as Swiveller and the little servant. The warmest upholder of Dickens would not go to the solemn or sentimental passages for anything fresh or suggestive in faith or philosophy. No one would pretend that the death of little Dombey (with its "What are the wild waves saying?") told us anything new or real about death. A good Christian dying, one would imagine, not only would not know what the wild waves were saying, but would not care. No one would pretend that the repentance of old Paul Dombey throws any light on the pyschology or philosophy of repentance. No doubt old Dombey, white-haired and amiable, was a great improvement on old Dombey brown-haired and unpleasant. But in his case the softening of the heart seems to bear too close a resemblance to softening of the brain. Whether these serious passages are as bad as the critical people or as good as the sentimental people find them, at least they do not convey anything in the way of an illuminating glimpse or a bold suggestion about men's moral nature. The serious figures do not tell one anything about the human soul. The comic figures do. Take anything almost at random out of these admirable speeches of Dick Swiveller. Notice, for instance, how exquisitely Dickens has caught a certain very deep and delicate quality at the bottom of this idle kind of man. I mean that odd impersonal sort of intellectual justice, by which the frivolous fellow sees things as they are and even himself as he is; and is above irritation. Mr. Swiveller, you remember, asks the Marchioness whether the Brass family ever talk about him; she nods her head with vivacity. " 'Complimentary?' inquired Mr. Swiveller. The motion of the little servant's head altered. . . . 'But she says,' continued the little servant, 'that you ain't to be trusted.' 'Well, do you know, Marchioness,' said Mr. Swiveller thoughtfully, 'many people, not exactly professional people, but tradesmen, have had the same idea. The excellent citizen from whom I ordered this beer inclines strongly to that opinion.' "

This philosophical freedom from all resentment, this strange love of truth which seems actually to come through carelessness, is a very real piece of spiritual observation. Even among liars there are two classes, one immeasurably better than another. The honest liar is the man who tells the truth about his old lies; who says on Wednesday, "I told a magnificent lie on Monday." He keeps the truth in circulation; no one version of things stagnates in him and becomes an evil secret. He does not have to live with old lies; a horrible domesticity. Mr. Swiveller may mislead the waiter about whether he has the money to pay; but he does not mislead his friend, and he does not mislead himself on the point. He is quite as well aware as any one can be of the accumulating falsity of the position of a gentleman who by his various debts has closed up all the streets into the Strand except one, and who is going to close that to-night with a pair of gloves.

He shuts up the street with a pair of gloves, but he does not shut up his mind with a secret. The traffic of truth is still kept open through his soul.

It is exactly in these absurd characters, then, that we can find a mass of psychological and ethical suggestion. This cannot be found in the serious characters except indeed in some of the later experiments: there is a little of such psychological and ethical suggestion in figures like Gridley, like Jasper, like Bradley Headstone. But in these earlier books at least, such as *The Old Curiosity Shop*, the grave or moral figures throw no light upon morals. I should maintain this generalisation even in the presence of that apparent exception *The Christmas Carol* with its trio of didactic ghosts. Charity is certainly splendid, at once a luxury and a necessity; but Dickens is not most effective when he is preaching charity seriously; he is most effective when he is preaching it uproariously; when he is preaching it by means of massive personalities and vivid scenes. One might say that he is best not when he is preaching his human love, but when he is practising it. In his grave pages he tells us to love men; but in his wild pages he creates men whom we can love. By his solemnity he commands us to love our neighbours. By his caricature he makes us love them.

There is an odd literary question which I wonder is not put more often in literature. How far can an author tell a truth without seeing it himself? Perhaps an actual example will express my meaning. I was once talking to a highly intelligent lady about Thackeray's *Newcomes*. We were speaking of the character of Mrs. Mackenzie, the Campaigner, and in the middle

of the conversation the lady leaned across to me and
said in a low, hoarse, but emphatic voice, "She drank.
Thackeray did n't know it; but she drank." And it is
really astonishing what a shaft of white light this
sheds on the Campaigner, on her terrible temperament, on her agonised abusiveness and her almost more
agonised urbanity, on her clamour which is nevertheless not open or explicable, on her temper which is not
so much bad temper as insatiable, bloodthirsty, man-
eating temper. How far can a writer thus indicate by
accident a truth of which he is himself ignorant? If
truth is a plan or pattern of things that really are, or
in other words, if truth truly exists outside ourselves,
or in other words, if truth exists at all, it must be often
possible for a writer to uncover a corner of it which he
happens not to understand, but which his reader does
happen to understand. The author sees only two
lines; the reader sees where they meet and what is the
angle. The author sees only an arc or fragment of a
curve; the reader sees the size of the circle. The last
thing to say about Dickens, and especially about books
like *The Old Curiosity Shop*, is that they are full of these
unconscious truths. The careless reader may miss
them. The careless author almost certainly did miss
them. But from them can be gathered an impression of
real truth to life which is for the grave critics of Dickens
an almost unknown benefit, buried treasure. Here
for instance is one of them out of *The Old Curiosity Shop*.
I mean the passage in which (by a blazing stroke of
genius) the dashing Mr. Chuckster, one of the Glorious
Apollos of whom Mr. Swiveller was the Perpetual Grand,
is made to entertain a hatred bordering upon frenzy

for the stolid, patient, respectful, and laborious Kit.
Now in the formal plan of the story Mr. Chuckster is
a fool, and Kit is almost a hero; at least he is a noble
boy. Yet unconsciously Dickens made the idiot
Chuckster say something profoundly suggestive on the
subject. In speaking of Kit Mr. Chuckster makes use
of these two remarkable phrases; that Kit is "meek"
and that he is "a snob." Now Kit is really a very fresh
and manly picture of a boy, firm, sane, chivalrous, reasonable, full of those three great Roman virtues which Mr.
Belloc has so often celebrated, *virtus* and *verecundia* and
pietas. He is a sympathetic but still a straightforward
study of the best type of that most respectable of all
human classes, the respectable poor. All this is true;
all that Dickens utters in praise of Kit is true; nevertheless the awful words of Chuckster remain written on
the eternal skies. Kit is meek and Kit is a snob. His
natural dignity does include and is partly marred by
that instinctive subservience to the employing class
which has been the comfortable weakness of the whole
English democracy, which has prevented their making
any revolution for the last two hundred years. Kit
would not serve any wicked man for money, but
he would serve any moderately good man and the
money would give a certain dignity and decisiveness to
the goodness. All this is the English popular evil which
goes along with the English popular virtues of geniality,
of homeliness, tolerance and strong humour, hope and
an enormous appetite for a hand-to-mouth happiness.
The scene in which Kit takes his family to the theatre
is a monument of the massive qualities of old English
enjoyment. If what we want is Merry England, our

antiquarians ought not to revive the Maypole or the Morris Dancers; they ought to revive Astley's and Sadler's Wells and the old solemn Circus and the old stupid Pantomime, and all the sawdust and all the oranges. Of all this strength and joy in the poor, Kit is a splendid and final symbol. But amid all his masculine and English virtue, he has this weak touch of meekness, or acceptance of the powers that be. It is a sound touch; it is a real truth about Kit. But Dickens did not know it. Mr. Chuckster did.

Dickens's stories taken as a whole have more artistic unity than appears at the first glance. It is the immediate impulse of a modern critic to dismiss them as mere disorderly scrap-books with very brilliant scraps. But this is not quite so true as it looks. In one of Dickens's novels there is generally no particular unity of construction; but there is often a considerable unity of sentiment and atmosphere. Things are irrelevant, but not somehow inappropriate. The whole book is written carelessly; but the whole book is generally written in one mood. To take a rude parallel from the other arts, we may say that there is not much unity of form, but there is much unity of colour. In most of the novels this can be seen. *Nicholas Nickleby*, as I have remarked, is full of a certain freshness, a certain light and open-air curiosity, which irradiates from the image of the young man swinging along the Yorkshire roads in the sun. Hence the comic characters with whom he falls in are comic characters in the same key; they are a band of strolling players, charlatans and poseurs, but too humane to be called humbugs. In the same way, the central story of

Oliver Twist is sombre; and hence even its comic character is almost sombre; at least he is too ugly to be merely amusing. Mr. Bumble is in some ways a terrible grotesque; his apoplectic visage recalls the "fire-red Cherubimme's face," which added such horror to the height and stature of Chaucer's Sompnour. In both these cases even the riotous and absurd characters are a little touched with the tint of the whole story. But this neglected merit of Dickens can certainly be seen best in *The Old Curiosity Shop*.

The curiosity shop itself was a lumber of grotesque and sinister things, outlandish weapons, twisted and diabolic decorations. The comic characters in the book are all like images bought in an old curiosity shop. Quilp might be a gargoyle. He might be some sort of devilish door-knocker, dropped down and crawling about the pavement. The same applies to the sinister and really terrifying stiffness of Sally Brass. She is like some old staring figure cut out of wood. Sampson Brass, her brother, again is a grotesque in the same rather inhuman manner; he is especially himself when he comes in with the green shade over his eye. About all this group of bad figures in *The Old Curiosity Shop* there is a sort of *diablerie*. There is also within this atmosphere an extraordinary energy of irony and laughter. The scene in which Sampson Brass draws up the description of Quilp, supposing him to be dead, reaches a point of fiendish fun. "We will not say very bandy, Mrs. Jiniwin," he says of his friend's legs, "we will confine ourselves to bandy. He is gone, my friends, where his legs would never be called in question." They go on to the discussion of his nose, and

Mrs. Jiniwin inclines to the view that it is flat. "Aquiline, you hag! Aquiline," cries Mr. Quilp, pushing in his head and striking his nose with his fist. There is nothing better in the whole brutal exuberance of the character than that gesture with which Quilp punches his own face with his own fist. It is indeed a perfect symbol; for Quilp is always fighting himself for want of anybody else. He is energy, and energy by itself is always suicidal; he is that primordial energy which tears and which destroys itself.

BARNABY RUDGE

Barnaby Rudge was written by Dickens in the spring and first flowing tide of his popularity; it came immediately after *The Old Curiosity Shop*, and only a short time after *Pickwick*. Dickens was one of those rare but often very sincere men in whom the high moment of success almost coincides with the high moment of youth. The calls upon him at this time were insistent and overwhelming; this necessarily happens at a certain stage of a successful writer's career. He was just successful enough to invite offers and not successful enough to reject them. At the beginning of his career he could throw himself into *Pickwick* because there was nothing else to throw himself into. At the end of his life he could throw himself into *A Tale of Two Cities*, because he refused to throw himself into anything else. But there was an intervening period, early in his life, when there was almost too much work for his imagination, and yet not quite enough work for his housekeeping. To this period *Barnaby Rudge* belongs. And it is a curious tribute to the quite curious greatness of Dickens that in this period of youthful strain we do not feel the strain but feel only the youth. His own amazing wish to write equalled or outstripped even his readers' amazing wish to read. Working too hard did not cure him of his abstract love of work. Unreasonable publishers asked him to write ten novels at once; but he wanted to write twenty novels at once. All this period is strangely full of his own sense at once of fertility and of futility; he did work which no one else could have done, and yet he could not be certain as yet that he was anybody.

Barnaby Rudge marks this epoch because it marks the fact that he is still confused about what kind of person he is going to be. He has already struck the note of the normal romance in *Nicholas Nickleby;* he has already created some of his highest comic characters in *Pickwick* and *The Old Curiosity Shop*, but here he betrays the fact that it is still a question what ultimate guide he shall follow. *Barnaby Rudge* is a romantic, historical novel. . Its design reminds us of Scott; some parts of its fulfilment remind us, alas! of Harrison Ainsworth. It is a very fine romantic historical novel; Scott would have been proud of it. But it is still so far different from the general work of Dickens that it is permissible to wonder how far Dickens was proud of it. The book, effective as it is, is almost entirely devoted to dealings with a certain artistic element, which (in its mere isolation) Dickens did not commonly affect; an element which many men of infinitely less genius have often seemed to affect more successfully; I mean the element of the picturesque.

It is the custom in many quarters to speak somewhat sneeringly of that element which is broadly called the picturesque. It is always felt to be an inferior, a vulgar, and even an artificial form of art. Yet two things may be remarked about it. The first is that, with few exceptions, the greatest literary artists have been not only particularly clever at the picturesque, but particularly fond of it. Shakespeare, for instance, delighted in certain merely pictorial contrasts which are quite distinct from, even when they are akin to, the spiritual view involved. For instance, there is admirable satire in the idea of Touchstone teaching worldly wisdom and worldly honour to the woodland yokels. There is excellent philosophy in the idea of the fool being the representative of civilisation in the forest. But quite apart from this deeper meaning in the incident, the mere figure of the jester, in his bright motley and his cap and bells, against the green background of the forest and the rude forms of the shepherds, is a strong example of the purely picturesque. There is excellent tragic irony in the confrontation of the melancholy philosopher among the tombs with the cheerful digger of the graves. It sums up the essential point, that dead bodies can be comic; it is only dead souls that can be tragic. But quite apart from such irony, the mere picture of the grotesque gravedigger, the black-clad prince, and the skull is a picture in the strongest sense picturesque. Caliban and the two shipwrecked drunkards are an admirable symbol; but they are also an admirable scene. Bottom, with the ass's head, sitting in a ring of elves, is excellent moving comedy, but also excellent still life. Falstaff with his huge body, Bardolph with his burning nose, are masterpieces of the pen; but they would be fine sketches even for the pencil. King Lear, in the storm, is a landscape as well as a character study. There is something decorative even about the insistence on the swarthiness of Othello, or the deformity of Richard III. Shakespeare's work is much more than picturesque; but it is picturesque. And the same which is said here of him by way of example is largely true of the highest class of literature. Dante's *Divine Comedy* is supremely important as a philosophy; but it is important merely as a panorama. Spenser's *Faery Queen* pleases us as an allegory; but it would please us even as a wall-paper. Stronger still is the case of Chaucer who loved the pure picturesque, which always includes something of what we commonly call the ugly. The huge stature and startling scarlet face of the Sompnour is in just the same spirit as Shakespeare's skulls and motley; the same spirit gave Chaucer's miller bagpipes, and clad his doctor in crimson. It is the spirit which, while making many other things, loves to make a picture.

Now the second thing to be remarked in apology for the picturesque is, that the very thing which makes it seem trivial ought really to make it seem important; I mean the fact that it consists necessarily of contrasts. It brings together types that stand out from their background, but are abruptly different from each other, like the clown among the fairies or the fool in the forest. And his audacious reconciliation is a mark not of frivolity but of extreme seriousness. A man who deals in harmonies, who only matches stars with angels or lambs with spring flowers, he indeed may be frivolous; for he is taking one mood at a time, and perhaps forgetting each mood as it passes. But a man who ventures to combine an angel and an octopus must have some serious view of the universe. The man who should write a dialogue between two early Christians might be a mere writer of dialogues. But a man who should write a dialogue between an early Christian and the Missing Link would have to be a philosopher. The more widely different the types talked of, the more serious and universal must be the philosophy which talks of them. The mark of the light and thoughtless writer is the harmony of his subject matter; the mark of the thoughtful writer is its apparent diversity. The most flippant lyric poet might write a pretty poem about lambs; but it requires something bolder and graver than a poet, it requires an ecstatic prophet, to talk about the lion lying down with the lamb.

Dickens, at any rate, strongly supports this conception: that great literary men as such do not despise the purely pictorial. No man's works have so much the quality of illustrating themselves. Few men's works have been more thoroughly and eagerly illustrated; few men's works can it have been better fun to illustrate. As a rule this fascinating quality in the mere fantastic figures of the tale was inseparable from their farcical quality in the tale. Stiggins's red nose is distinctly connected with the fact that he is a member of the Ebenezer Temperance Association; Quilp is little, because a little of him goes a long way. Mr. Carker smiles and smiles and is a villain; Mr. Chadband is fat because in his case to be fat is to be hated. The story is immeasurably more important than the picture; it is not mere indulgence in the picturesque. Generally it is an intellectual love of the comic; not a pure love of the grotesque.

But in one book Dickens suddenly confesses that he

likes the grotesque even without the comic. In one case he makes clear that he enjoys pure pictures with a pure love of the picturesque. That place is *Barnaby Rudge*. There had indeed been hints of it in many episodes in his books; notably, for example, in that fine scene of the death of Quilp—a scene in which the dwarf remains fantastic long after he has ceased to be in any way funny. Still, the dwarf was meant to be funny. Humour of a horrible kind, but still humour, is the purpose of Quilp's existence and position in the book. Laughter is the object of all his oddities. But laughter is not the object of Barnaby Rudge's oddities. His idiot costume and his ugly raven are used for the purpose of the pure grotesque; solely to make a certain kind of Gothic sketch.

It is commonly this love of pictures that drives men back upon the historical novel. But it is very typical of Dickens's living interest in his own time, that though he wrote two historical novels they were neither of them of very ancient history. They were both, indeed, of very recent history; only they were those parts of recent history which were specially picturesque. I do not think that this was due to any mere consciousness on his part that he knew no history. Undoubtedly he knew no history; and he may or may not have been conscious of the fact. But the consciousness did not prevent him from writing a *History of England*. Nor did it prevent him from interlarding all or any of his works with tales of the pictorial past, such as the tale of the broken swords in *Master Humphrey's Clock*, or the indefensibly delightful nightmare of the lady in the stage-coach, which helps to soften the amiable end

of Pickwick. Neither, worst of all, did it prevent him
from dogmatising anywhere and everywhere about
the past, of which he knew nothing; it did not prevent
him from telling the bells to tell Trotty Veck that the
Middle Ages were a failure, nor from solemnly declaring
that the best thing that the mediæval monks ever did
was to create the mean and snobbish quietude of a
modern cathedral city. No, it was not historical
reverence that held him back from dealing with the
remote past; but rather something much better—a
living interest in the living century in which he was
born. He would have thought himself quite intel-
lectually capable of writing a novel about the Council
of Trent or the First Crusade. He would have thought
himself quite equal to analysing the psychology of
Abelard or giving a bright, satiric sketch of St. Augustine. It must frankly be confessed that it was not a
sense of his own unworthiness that held him back; I
fear it was rather a sense of St. Augustine's unworthiness. He could not see the point of any history before
the first slow swell of the French Revolution. He could
understand the revolutions of the eighteenth century;
all the other revolutions of history (so many and so
splendid) were unmeaning to him. But the revolutions
of the eighteenth century he did understand; and to
them therefore he went back, as all historical novelists
go back, in search of the picturesque. And from this
fact an important result follows.

The result that follows is this: that his only two
historical novels are both tales of revolutions—of
eighteenth-century revolutions. These two eighteenth-
century revolutions may seem to differ, and perhaps

do differ in everything except in being revolutions and of the eighteenth century. The French Revolution, which is the theme of *A Tale of Two Cities*, was a revolt in favour of all that is now called enlightenment and liberation. The great Gordon Riot, which is the theme of *Barnaby Rudge*, was a revolt in favour of something which would now be called mere ignorant and obscurantist Protestantism. Nevertheless both belonged more typically to the age out of which Dickens came—the great sceptical and yet creative eighteenth century of Europe. Whether the mob rose on the right side or the wrong they both belonged to the time in which a mob could rise, in which a mob could conquer. No growth of intellectual science or of moral cowardice had made it impossible to fight in the streets, whether for the republic or for the Bible. If we wish to know what was the real link, existing actually in ultimate truth, existing unconsciously in Dickens's mind, which connected the Gordon Riots with the French Revolution, the link may be defined though not with any great adequacy. The nearest and truest way of stating it is that neither of the two could possibly happen in Fleet Street to-morrow evening.

Another point of resemblance between the two books might be found in the fact that they both contain the sketch of the same kind of eighteenth-century aristocrat, if indeed that kind of aristocrat really existed in the eighteenth century. The diabolical dandy with the rapier and the sneer is at any rate a necessity of all normal plays and romances; hence Mr. Chester has a right to exist in this romance, and Foulon a right to exist in a page of history almost as cloudy and disputable as a romance. What Dickens and other romancers do probably omit from the picture of the eighteenth-century oligarch is probably his liberality. It must never be forgotten that even when he was a despot in practice he was generally a liberal in theory. Dickens and romancers make the pre-revolution tyrant a sincere believer in tyranny; generally he was not. He was a sceptic about everything, even about his own position. The romantic Foulon says of the people, "Let them eat grass," with bitter and deliberate contempt. The real Foulon (if he ever said it at all) probably said it as a sort of dreary joke because he could n't think of any other way out of the problem. Similiarly Mr. Chester, a cynic as he is, believes seriously in the beauty of being a gentleman; a real man of that type probably disbelieved in that as in everything else. Dickens was too bracing, one may say too bouncing himself to understand the psychology of fatigue in a protected and leisured class. He could understand a tyrant like Quilp, a tyrant who is on his throne because he has climbed up into it, like a monkey. He could not understand a tyrant who is on his throne because he is too weary to get out of it. The old aristocrats were in a dead way quite good-natured. They were even humanitarians; which perhaps accounts for the extent to which they roused against themselves the healthy hatred of humanity. But they were tired humanitarians; tired with doing nothing. Figures like that of Mr. Chester, therefore, fail somewhat to give the true sense of something hopeless and helpless which led men to despair of the upper class. He has a boyish pleasure in play-acting; he has an interest in life; being

a villain is his hobby. But the true man of that type
had found all hobbies fail him. He had wearied of
himself as he had wearied of a hundred women. He
was graceful and could not even admire himself in the
glass. He was witty and could not even laugh at his
own jokes. Dickens could never understand tedium.

There is no mark more strange and perhaps sinister
of the interesting and not very sane condition of our
modern literature, than the fact that tedium has been
admirably described in it. Our best modern writers
are never so exciting as they are about dulness. Mr.
Rudyard Kipling is never so powerful as when he is
painting yawning deserts, aching silences, sleepless
nights, or infernal isolation. The excitement in one
of the stories of Mr. Henry James becomes tense,
thrilling, and almost intolerable in all the half hours
during which nothing whatever is said or done. We
are entering again into the mind, into the real mind
of Foulon and Mr. Chester. We begin to understand
the deep despair of those tyrants whom our fathers
pulled down. But Dickens could never have understood that despair; it was not in his soul. And it is
an interesting coincidence that here, in this book of
Barnaby Rudge, there is a character meant to be wholly
grotesque, who, nevertheless, expresses much of that
element in Dickens which prevented him from being a
true interpreter of the tired and sceptical aristocrat.

Sim Tappertit is a fool, but a perfectly honourable
fool. It requires some sincerity to pose. Posing
means that one has not dried up in oneself all the
youthful and innocent vanities with the slow paralysis
of mere pride. Posing means that one is still fresh

enough to enjoy the good opinion of one's fellows.
On the other hand, the true cynic has not enough truth
in him to attempt affectation; he has never even seen
the truth, far less tried to imitate it. Now we might
very well take the type of Mr. Chester on the one hand,
and of Sim Tappertit on the other, as marking the
issue, the conflict, and the victory which really ushered
in the nineteenth century. Dickens was very like Sim
Tappertit. The Liberal Revolution was very like a
Sim Tappertit revolution. It was vulgar, it was over-
done, it was absurd, but it was alive. Dickens was
vulgar, was absurd, overdid everything, but he was alive.
The aristocrats were perfectly correct, but quite dead;
dead long before they were guillotined. The classics
and critics who lamented that Dickens was no gentleman were quite right, but quite dead. The revolution
thought itself rational; but so did Sim Tappertit. It
was really a huge revolt of romanticism against a
reason which had grown sick even of itself. Sim
Tappertit rose against Mr. Chester; and, thank God!
he put his foot upon his neck.

AMERICAN NOTES

American Notes was written soon after Dickens had returned from his first visit to America. That visit had, of course, been a great epoch in his life; but how much of an epoch men did not truly realise until, some time after, in the middle of a quiet story about Salisbury and a ridiculous architect, his feelings flamed out and flared up to the stars in *Martin Chuzzlewit*. The *American Notes* are, however, interesting, because in them he betrays his feelings when he does not know that he is betraying them. Dickens's first visit to America was, from his own point of view, and at the beginning, a happy and festive experiment. It is very characteristic of him that he went among the Americans, enjoyed them, even admired them, and then had a quarrel with them. Nothing was ever so unmistakable as his good-will, except his ill-will; and they were never far apart. And this was not, as some bloodless moderns have sneeringly insinuated, a mere repetition of the proximity between the benevolent stage and the quarrelsome stage of drink. It was a piece of pure optimism; he believed so readily that men were going to be good to him that an injury to him was something more than an injury: it was a shock. What was the exact nature of the American shock must, however, be more carefully stated.

The famous quarrel between Dickens and America, which finds its most elaborate expression in *American Notes*, though its most brilliant expression in *Martin Chuzzlewit*, is an incident about which a great deal remains to be said. But the thing which most specially remains to be said is this. This old Anglo-American quarrel was much more fundamentally friendly than most Anglo-American alliances. In Dickens's day each nation understood the other enough to argue. In our time neither nation understands itself even enough to quarrel. There was an English tradition, from Fox and eighteenth-century England; there was an American tradition from Franklin and eighteenth-century America; and they were still close enough together to discuss their differences with acrimony, perhaps, but with certain fundamental understandings. The eighteenth-century belief in a liberal civilisation was still a dogma; for dogma is the only thing that makes argument or reasoning possible. America, under all its swagger, did still really believe that Europe was its fountain and its mother, because Europe was more fully civilised. Dickens, under all his disgust, did still believe that America was in advance of Europe, because it was more democratic. It was an age, in short, in which the word "progress" could still be used reasonably; because the whole world looked to one way of escape and there was only one kind of progress under discussion. Now, of course, "progress" is a useless word; for progress takes for granted an already defined direction; and it is exactly about the direction that we disagree. Do not let us therefore be misled into any mistaken optimism or special self-congratulation

upon what many people would call the improved relations between England and America.   The relations are
improved because America has finally become a foreign
country.   And with foreign countries all sane men take
care to exchange a certain consideration and courtesy.
But even as late as the time of Dickens's first visit to
the United States, we English still felt America as a
colony; an insolent, offensive, and even unintelligible
colony sometimes, but still a colony; a part of our
civilisation, a limb of our life.   And America itself,
as I have said, under all its bounce and independence,
really regarded us as a mother country.   This being
the case it was possible for us to quarrel, like kinsmen.
Now we only bow and smile, like strangers.

   This tone, as a sort of family responsibility, can be
felt quite specially all through the satires or suggestions
of these *American Notes*.   Dickens is cross with
America because he is worried about America; as if
he were its father.   He explores its industrial, legal,
and educational arrangements like a mother looking
at the housekeeping of a married son; he makes suggestions with a certain acidity; he takes a strange
pleasure in being pessimistic.   He advises them to
take note of how much better certain things are done
in England.   All this is very different from Dickens's
characteristic way of dealing with a foreign country.
In countries really foreign, such as France, Switzer-
land, and Italy, he had two attitudes, neither of them
in the least worried or paternal.   When he found a
thing in Europe which he did not understand, such as
the Roman Catholic Church, he simply called it an old-
world superstition, and sat looking at it like a moonlit

ruin. When he found something that he did understand, such as luncheon baskets, he burst into carols of praise over the superior sense in our civilisation and good management to Continental methods. An example of the first attitude may be found in one of his letters, in which he describes the backwardness and idleness of Catholics who would not build a Birmingham in Italy. He seems quite unconscious of the obvious truth, that the backwardness of Catholics was simply the refusal of Bob Cratchit to enter the house of Gradgrind. An example of the second attitude can be found in the purple patches of fun in *Mugby Junction;* in which the English waitress denounces the profligate French habit of providing new bread and clean food for people travelling by rail. The point is, however, that in neither case has he the air of one suggesting improvements or sharing a problem with the people engaged on it. He does not go carefully with a notebook through Jesuit schools nor offer friendly suggestions to the governors of Parisian prisons. Or if he does, it is in a different spirit; it is in the spirit of an ordinary tourist being shown over the Coliseum or the Pyramids. But he visited America in the spirit of a Government inspector dealing with something it was his duty to inspect. This is never felt either in his praise or blame of Continental countries. When he did not leave a foreign country to decay like a dead dog, he merely watched it at play like a kitten. France he mistook for a kitten. Italy he mistook for a dead dog.

But with America he could feel—and fear. There he could hate, because he could love. There he could feel not the past alone nor the present, but the future also; and, like all brave men, when he saw the future he was a little afraid of it. For of all tests by which the good citizen and strong reformer can be distinguished from the vague faddist or the inhuman sceptic, I know no better test than this—that the unreal reformer sees in front of him one certain future, the future of his fad; while the real reformer sees before him ten or twenty futures among which his country must choose, and may, in some dreadful hour, choose the wrong one. The true patriot is always doubtful of victory; because he knows that he is dealing with a living thing; a thing with free will. To be certain of free will is to be uncertain of success.

The subject matter of the real difference of opinion between Dickens and the public of America can only be understood if it is thus treated as a dispute between brothers about the destiny of a common heritage. The point at issue might be stated like this. Dickens, on his side, did not in his heart doubt for a moment that England would eventually follow America along the road towards real political equality and purely republican institutions. He lived, it must be remembered, before the revival of aristocracy, which has since overwhelmed us—the revival of aristocracy worked through popular science and commercial dictatorship, and which has nowhere been more manifest than in America itself. He knew nothing of this; in his heart he conceded to the Yankees that not only was their revolution right but would ultimately be completed everywhere. But on the other hand, his whole point against the American experiment was this—that if it ignored certain ancient

English contributions it would go to pieces for lack of them. Of these the first was good manners and the second individual liberty—liberty, that is, to speak and write against the trend of the majority. In these things he was much more serious and much more sensible than it is the fashion to think he was; he was indeed one of the most serious and sensible critics England ever had of current and present problems, though his criticism is useless to the point of nonentity about all things remote from him in style of civilisation or in time. His point about good manners is really important. All his grumblings through this book of *American Notes*, all his shrieking satire in *Martin Chuzzlewit* are expressions of a grave and reasonable fear he had touching the future of democracy. And remember again what has been already remarked—instinctively he paid America the compliment of looking at her as the future of democracy.

The mistake which he attacked still exists. I cannot imagine why it is that social equality is somehow supposed to mean social familiarity. Why should equality mean that all men are equally rude? Should it not rather mean that all men are equally polite? Might it not quite reasonably mean that all men should be equally ceremonious and stately and pontifical? What is there specially Equalitarian, for instance, in calling your political friends and even your political enemies by their Christian names in public? There is something very futile in the way in which certain Socialist leaders call each other Tom, Dick, and Harry; especially when Tom is accusing Harry of having basely imposed upon the well-known imbecility of Dick. There is something quite undemocratic in all men calling each other by the special and affectionate term "comrade"; especially when they say it with a sneer and smart inquiry about the funds. Democracy would be quite satisfied if every man called every other man "sir." Democracy would have no conceivable reason to complain if every man called every other man "your excellency" or "your holiness" or "brother of the sun and moon." The only democratic essential is that it should be a term of dignity and that it should be given to all. To abolish all terms of dignity is no more specially democratic than the Roman emperor's wish to cut off everybody's head at once was specially democratic. That involved equality certainly, but it was lacking in respect.

Dickens saw America as markedly the seat of this danger. He saw that there was a perilous possibility that republican ideals might be allied to a social anarchy good neither for them nor for any other ideals. Republican simplicity, which is difficult, might be quickly turned into Bohemian brutality, which is easy. Cincinnatus, instead of putting his hand to the plough, might put his feet on the tablecloth, and an impression prevail that it was all a part of the same rugged equality and freedom. Insolence might become a tradition. Bad manners might have all the sanctity of good manners. "There you are!" cries Martin Chuzzlewit indignantly, when the American has befouled the butter. "A man deliberately makes a hog of himself and *that* is an Institution." But the thread of thought which we must always keep in hand in this matter is that he would not thus have worried about the degrada-

tion of republican simplicity into general rudeness if
he had not from first to last instinctively felt that
America held human democracy in her hand, to exalt
it or to let it fall. In one of his gloomier moments he
wrote down his fear that the greatest blow ever struck
at liberty would be struck by America in the failure
of her mission upon the earth.

This brings us to the other ground of his alarm—the
matter of liberty of speech. Here also he was much
more reasonable and philosophic than has commonly
been realised. The truth is that the lurid individualism of Carlyle has, with its violent colours, "killed"
the tones of most criticism of his time; and just as we
can often see a scheme of decoration better if we cover
some flaming picture, so you can judge nineteenth-
century England much better if you leave Carlyle out.
He is important to moderns because he led that return
to Toryism which has been the chief feature of modernity, but his judgments were often not only spiritually
false, but really quite superficial. Dickens understood
the danger of democracy far better than Carlyle; just
as he understood the merits of democracy far better
than Carlyle. And of this fact we can produce one
plain evidence in the matter of which we speak. Carlyle,
in his general dislike of the revolutionary movement,
lumped liberty and democracy together and said that
the chief objection to democracy was that it involved
the excess and misuse of liberty; he called democracy
"anarchy or no-rule." Dickens, with far more philosophical insight and spiritual delicacy, saw that the
real danger of democracy is that it tends to the very
opposite of anarchy; even to the very opposite of liberty.

He lamented in America the freedom of manners.
But he lamented even more the absence of freedom of
opinion. "I believe there is no country on the face
of the earth," he says, "where there is less freedom of
opinion on any subject in reference to which there is
a broad difference of opinion than in this. There!
I write the words with reluctance, disappointment,
and sorrow; but I believe it from the bottom of my
soul. The notion that I, a man alone by myself in
America, should venture to suggest to the Americans
that there was one point on which they were neither
just to their own countrymen nor to us, actually
struck the boldest dumb! Washington Irving, Prescott,
Hoffman, Bryant, Halleck, Dana, Washington Allston
—every man who writes in this country is devoted to
the question, and not one of them *dares* to raise his
voice and complain of the atrocious state of the law.
The wonder is that a breathing man can be found
with temerity enough to suggest to the Americans the
possibility of their having done wrong. I wish you
could have seen the faces that I saw down both sides of
the table at Hartford when I began to talk about Scott.
I wish you could have heard how I gave it out. My
blood so boiled when I thought of the monstrous injustice that I felt as if I were twelve feet high when
I thrust it down their throats." Dickens knew no
history, but he had all history behind him in feeling
that a pure democracy does tend, when it goes wrong,
to be too traditional and absolute. The truth is indeed
a singular example of the unfair attack upon democracy
in our own time. Everybody can repeat the platitude
that the mob can be the greatest of all tyrants. But

few realise or remember the corresponding truth which goes along with it—that the mob is the only permanent and unassailable high priest. Democracy drives its traditions too hard; but democracy is the only thing that keeps any traditions. An aristocracy must always be going after some new thing. The severity of democracy is far more of a virtue than its liberty. The decorum of a democracy is far more of a danger than its lawlessness. Dickens discovered this in his great quarrels about the copyright, when a whole nation acted on a small point of opinion as if it were going to lynch him. But, fortunately for the purpose of this argument, there is no need to go back to the forties for such a case. Another great literary man has of late visited America; and it is possible that Maxim Gorky may be in a position to state how far democracy is likely to err on the side of mere liberty and laxity. He may have found, like Dickens, some freedom of manners; he did not find much freedom of morals.

Along with such American criticism should really go his very characteristic summary of the question of the Red Indian. It marks the combination between the mental narrowness and the moral justice of the old Liberal. Dickens can see nothing in the Red Indian except that he is barbaric, retrograde, bellicose, uncleanly, and superstitious—in short, that he is not a member of the special civilisation of Birmingham or Brighton. It is curious to note the contrast between the cheery, nay Cockney, contempt with which Dickens speaks of the American Indian and that chivalrous and pathetic essay in which Washington Irving celebrates the virtues of the vanishing race. Between Washington

Irving and his friend Charles Dickens there was always indeed this ironical comedy of inversion. It is amusing that the Englishman should have been the pushing and even pert modernist, and the American the stately antiquarian and lover of lost causes. But while a man of more mellòw sympathies may well dislike Dickens's dislike of savages, and even disdain his disdain, he ought to sharply remind himself of the admirable ethical fairness and equity which meet with that restricted outlook. In the very act of describing Red Indians as devils who, like so much dirt, it would pay us to sweep away, he pauses to deny emphatically that we have any right to sweep them away. We have no right to wrong the man, he means to say, even if he himself be a kind of wrong. Here we strike the ringing iron of the old conscience and sense of honour which marked the best men of his party and of his epoch. This rigid and even reluctant justice towers, at any rate, far above modern views of savages, above the sentimentalism of the mere humanitarian and the far weaker sentimentalism that pleads for brutality and a race war. Dickens was at least more of a man than the brutalitarian who claims to wrong people because they are nasty, or the humanitarian who cannot be just to them without pretending that they are nice.

PICTURES FROM ITALY

THE *Pictures from Italy* are excellent in themselves and excellent as a foil to the *American Notes*. Here we have none of that air of giving a decision like a judge or sending in a report like an inspector; here we have only glimpses, light and even fantastic glimpses, of a world that is really alien to Dickens. It is so alien that he can almost entirely enjoy it. For no man can entirely enjoy that which he loves; contentment is always unpatriotic. The difference can indeed be put with approximate perfection in one phrase. In Italy he was on a holiday; in America he was on a tour. But indeed Dickens himself has quite sufficiently conveyed the difference in the two phrases that he did actually use for the titles of the two books. Dickens often told unconscious truths, especially in small matters. The *American Notes* really are notes, like the notes of a student or a professional witness. The *Pictures from Italy* are only pictures from Italy, like the miscellaneous pictures that all tourists bring from Italy.

To take another and perhaps closer figure of speech, almost all Dickens's works such as these may best be regarded as private letters addressed to the public. His private correspondence was quite as brilliant as his public works; and many of his public works are almost as formless and casual as his private correspondence.

If he had been struck insensible for a year, I really think that his friends and family could have brought out one of his best books by themselves if they had happened to keep his letters. The homogeneity of his public and private work was indeed strange in many ways. On the one hand, there was little that was pompously and unmistakably public in the publications; on the other hand, there was very little that was private in the private letters. His hilarity had almost a kind of hardness about it; no man's letters, I should think, ever needed less expurgation on the ground of weakness or undue confession. The main part, and certainly the best part, of such a book as *Pictures from Italy* can certainly be criticised best as part of that perpetual torrent of entertaining autobiography which he flung at his children as if they were his readers and his readers as if they were his children. There are some brilliant patches of sense and nonsense in this book; but there is always something accidental in them; as if they might have occurred somewhere else. Perhaps the most attractive of them is the incomparable description of the Italian Marionette Theatre in which they acted a play about the death of Napoleon in St. Helena. The description is better than that of Codlin and Short's Punch and Judy, and almost as good as that of Mrs. Jarley's Wax Works. Indeed the humour is similar; for Punch is supposed to be funny, but Napoleon (as Mrs. Jarley said when asked if her show was funnier than Punch) was not funny at all. The idea of a really tragic scene being enacted between tiny wooden dolls with large heads is delightfully dealt with by Dickens. We can almost imagine

the scene in which the wooden Napoleon haughtily
rebukes his wooden jailor for calling him General Bona-
parte—"Sir Hudson Low, call me not thus; I am
Napoleon, Emperor of the French." There is also
something singularly gratifying about the scene of
Napoleon's death, in which he lay in bed with his little
wooden hands outside the counterpane and the doctor
(who was hung on wires too short) "delivered medical
opinions in the air." It may seem flippant to dwell
on such flippancies in connection with a book which
contains many romantic descriptions and many moral
generalisations which Dickens probably valued highly.
But it is not for such things that he is valued. In all
his writings, from his most reasoned and sustained
novel to his maddest private note, it is always this
obstreperous instinct for farce which stands out as his
in the highest sense. His wisdom is at the best talent,
his foolishness is genius. Just that exuberant levity
which we associate with a moment we associate in his
case with immortality. It is said of certain old ma-
sonry that the mortar was so hard that it has survived
the stones. So if Dickens could revisit the thing he
built, he would be surprised to see all the work he
thought solid and responsible wasted almost utterly
away, but the shortest frivolities and the most momentary jokes remaining like colossal rocks for ever.

MARTIN CHUZZLEWIT

THERE is a certain quality or element which broods over the whole of *Martin Chuzzlewit* to which it is difficult for either friends or foes to put a name. I think the reader who enjoys Dickens's other books has an impression that it is a kind of melancholy. There are grotesque figures of the most gorgeous kind; there are scenes that are farcical even by the standard of the farcical license of Dickens; there is humour both of the heaviest and of the lightest kind; there are two great comic personalities who run like a rich vein through the whole story, Pecksniff and Mrs. Gamp; there is one blinding patch of brilliancy, the satire on American cant; there is Todgers's boarding-house; there is Bailey; there is Mr. Mould, the incomparable undertaker. But yet in spite of everything, in spite even of the undertaker, the book is sad. No one I think ever went to it in that mixed mood of a tired tenderness and a readiness to believe and laugh in which most of Dickens's novels are most enjoyed. We go for a particular novel to Dickens as we go for a particular inn. We go to the sign of the Pickwick Papers. We go to the sign of the Rudge and Raven. We go to the sign of the Old Curiosities. We go to the sign of the Two Cities. We go to each or all of them according to what kind of hospitality and what kind of happiness we require. But it is always some kind of hospitality and some kind of happiness that we require. And as in the case of inns we also remember that while there was shelter in all and food in all and some kind of fire and some kind of wine in all, yet one has left upon us an indescribable and unaccountable memory of mortality and decay, of dreariness in the rooms and even of tastelessness in the banquet. So any one who has enjoyed the stories of Dickens as they should be enjoyed has a nameless feeling that this one story is sad and almost sodden. Dickens himself had this feeling, though his breezy vanity forbade him to express it in so many words. In spite of Pecksniff, in spite of Mrs. Gamp, in spite of the yet greater Bailey, the story went lumberingly and even lifelessly; he found the sales falling off; he fancied his popularity waning, and by a sudden impulse most inartistic and yet most artistic, he dragged in the episode of Martin's visit to America, which is the blazing jewel and the sudden redemption of the book. He wrote it at an uneasy and unhappy period of his life; when he had ceased wandering in America, but could not cease wandering altogether; when he had lost his original routine of work which was violent but regular, and had not yet settled down to the full enjoyment of his success and his later years. He poured into this book genius that might make the mountains laugh, invention that juggled with the stars. But the book was sad; and he knew it.

The just reason for this is really interesting. Yet it is one that is not easy to state without guarding one's self on the one side or the other against great misunderstandings; and these stipulations or preliminary allowances must in such a case as this of necessity be made first. Dickens was among other things a satirist, a pure satirist. I have never been able to understand why this title is always specially and sacredly reserved for Thackeray. Thackeray was a novelist; in the strict and narrow sense at any rate, Thackeray was a far greater novelist than Dickens. But Dickens certainly was the satirist. The essence of satire is that it perceives some absurdity inherent in the logic of some position, and that it draws that absurdity out and isolates it, so that all can see it. Thus for instance when Dickens says, "Lord Coodle would go out; Sir Thomas Doodle would n't come in; and there being no people to speak of in England except Coodle and Doodle the country has been without a Government"; when Dickens says this he suddenly pounces on and plucks out the one inherent absurdity in the English party system which is hidden behind all its paraphernalia of Parliaments and Statutes, elections and ballot papers. When all the dignity and all the patriotism and all the public interest of the English constitutional party conflict have been fully allowed for, there does remain the bold, bleak question which Dickens in substance asks, "Suppose I want somebody else who is neither Coodle nor Doodle." This is the great quality called satire; it is a kind of taunting reasonableness; and it is inseparable from a certain insane logic which is often called exaggeration. Dickens was more of a satirist than Thackeray for this simple reason: that Thackeray carried a man's principles as far as that man carried them; Dickens carried a man's principles as far as a man's principles would go. Dickens in short (as people put it) exaggerated the man and his principles; that is to say he emphasised them. Dickens drew a man's absurdity out of him; Thackeray left a man's absurdity in him. Of this last fact we can take any example we like; take for instance the comparison between the city man as treated by Thackeray in the most satiric of his novels, with the city man as treated by Dickens in one of the mildest and maturest of his. Compare the character of old Mr. Osborne in *Vanity Fair* with the character of Mr. Podsnap in *Our Mutual Friend*. In the case of Mr. Osborne there is nothing except the solid blocking in of a brutal dull convincing character. *Vanity Fair* is not a satire on the City except in so far as it happens to be true. *Vanity Fair* is not a satire on the City, in short, except in so far as the City is a satire on the City. But Mr. Podsnap is a pure satire; he is an extracting out of the City man of those purely intellectual qualities which happen to make that kind of City man a particularly exasperating fool. One might almost say that Mr. Podsnap is all Mr. Osborne's opinions separated from Mr. Osborne and turned into a character. In short the satirist is more purely philosophical than the novelist. The novelist may be only an observer; the satirist must be a thinker. He must be a thinker, he must be a philosophical thinker for this simple reason; that he exercises his philosophical thought in deciding what part of his subject he is to satirise. You may have the dullest possible intelligence and be a portrait painter; but a man must have a serious intellect in order to be a caricaturist. He has to select what thing he will caricature. True satire is always of this intellectual kind; true satire is always, so to speak, a variation or fantasia upon the air of pure logic. The satirist is the man who carries men's enthusiasm further than they carry it themselves. He outstrips the most extravagant fanatic. He is years ahead of the most audacious prophet. He sees where men's detached intellect will eventually lead them, and he tells them the name of the place—which is generally hell.

Now of this detached and rational use of satire there is one great example in this book. Even *Gulliver's Travels* is hardly more reasonable than Martin Chuzzlewit's travels in the incredible land of the Americans. Before considering the humour of this description in its more exhaustive and liberal aspects, it may be first remarked that in this American part of *Martin Chuzzlewit*, Dickens quite specially sharpens up his own mere controversial and political intelligence. There are more things here than anywhere else in Dickens that partake of the nature of pamphleteering, of positive challenge, of sudden repartee, of pugnacious and exasperating query, in a word of everything that belongs to the pure art of controversy as distinct not only from the pure art of fiction but even also from the pure art of satire. I am inclined to think (to put the matter not only shortly but clumsily) that Dickens was never in all his life so strictly clever as he is in the American part of *Martin Chuzzlewit*. There are places where he was more inspired, almost in the sense of being intoxicated, as, for instance, in the Micawber feasts of *David Copperfield;* there are places where he wrote more carefully and cunningly, as, for instance, in the mystery of *The Mystery of Edwin Drood;* there are places where he wrote very much more humanly, more close to the ground and to growing things, as in the whole of that admirable book *Great Expectations*. But I do not think that his mere abstract acuteness and rapidity of thought were ever exercised with such startling exactitude as they are in this place in *Martin Chuzzlewit*. It is to be noted, for instance, that his American experience had actually worked him up to a heat and habit of argument. A slave-owner in the Southern States tells Dickens that slave-owners do not ill-treat their slaves, that it is not to the interest of slave-owners to ill-treat their slaves. Dickens flashes back that it is not to the interest of a man to get drunk, but he does get drunk. This pugnacious atmosphere of parry and riposte must first of all be allowed for and understood in all the satiric excursus of Martin in America. Dickens is arguing all the time; and, to do him justice, arguing very well. These chapters are full not merely of exuberant satire on America in the sense that Dotheboys Hall or Mr. Bumble's Workhouse are exuberant satires on England. They are full also of sharp argument with America as if the man who wrote expected retort and was prepared with rejoinder. The rest of the book, like the rest of Dickens's books, possesses humour. This part of the book, like hardly any of Dickens's books, possesses wit. The republican gentleman who receives Martin on landing is horrified on hearing an English servant speak of the employer as "the master." "There are no masters in America," says the gentleman. "All owners are they?" says Martin. This sort of verbal promptitude is out of the ordinary scope of Dickens; but we find it frequently

in this particular part of *Martin Chuzzlewit*. Martin
himself is constantly breaking out into a controversial
lucidity, which is elsewhere not at all a part of his
character. When they talk to him about the institutions of America he asks sarcastically whether bowie
knives and swordsticks and revolvers are the institutions of America. All this (if I may summarise) is
expressive of one main fact. Being a satirist means
being a philosopher. Dickens was not always very
philosophical; but he had this permanent quality of
the philosopher about him, that he always remembered
people by their opinions. Elijah Pogram was to him
the man who said that "his boastful answer to the
tyrant and the despot was that his bright home was
the land of the settin' sun." Mr. Scadder and Mr.
Jefferson Brick were to him the men who said (in co-
operation) that "the libation of freedom must sometimes be quaffed in blood." And in these chapters
more than anywhere else he falls into the extreme habit
of satire, that of treating people as if there were nothing
about them except their opinions. It is therefore difficult to accept these pages as pages in a novel, splendid
as they are considered as pages in a parody. I do not
dispute that men have said and do say that "the
libation of freedom must sometimes be quaffed in
blood," that "their bright homes are the land of the
settin' sun," that "they taunt that lion," that "alone
they dare him," or "that softly sleeps the calm ideal
in the whispering chambers of imagination." I have
read too much American journalism to deny that any
of these sentences and any of these opinions may at
some time or other have been uttered. I do not deny

that there are such opinions. But I do deny that
there are such people. Elijah Pogram had some other
business in life besides defending defaulting post-
masters; he must have been a son or a father or a
husband or at least (admirable thought) a lover. Mr.
Chollop had some moments in his existence when he
was not threatening his fellow-creatures with his sword-
stick and his revolver. Of all this human side of
such American types Dickens does not really give any
hint at all. He does not suggest that the bully Chollop
had even such coarse good-humour as bullies almost
always have. He does not suggest that the humbug
Elijah Pogram had even as much greasy amiability
as humbugs almost invariably have. He is not studying them as human beings, even as bad human beings;
he is studying them as conceptions, as points of view, as
symbols of a state of mind with which he is in violent
disagreement. To put it roughly, he is not describing
characters, he is satirising fads. To put it more exactly,
he is not describing characters; he is persecuting
heresies. There is one thing really to be said against
his American satire; it is a serious thing to be said: it is
an argument, and it is true. This can be said of
Martin's wanderings in America, that from the time
he lands in America to the time he sets sail from it he
never meets a living man. He has travelled in the
land of Laputa. All the people he has met have
been absurd opinions walking about. The whole art
of Dickens in such passages as these consisted in one
thing. It consisted in finding an opinion that had not
a leg to stand on, and then giving it two legs to stand
on.

So much may be allowed; it may be admitted that Dickens is in this sense the great satirist, in that he can imagine absurd opinions walking by themselves about the street. It may be admitted that Thackeray would not have allowed an absurd opinion to walk about the street without at least tying a man on to it for the sake of safety. But while this first truth may be evident, the second truth which is the complement of it may easily be forgotten. On the one hand there was no man who could so much enjoy mere intellectual satire apart from humanity as Dickens. On the other hand there was no man who, with another and more turbulent part of his nature, demanded humanity, and demanded its supremacy over intellect, more than Dickens. To put it shortly: there never was a man so much fitted for saying that everything was wrong; and there never was a man who was so desirous of saying that everything was right. Thus, when he met men with whom he violently disagreed, he described them as devils or lunatics; he could not bear to describe them as men. If they could not think with him on essentials he could not stand the idea that they were human souls; he cast them out; he forgot them; and if he could not forget them he caricatured them. He was too emotional to regard them as anything but enemies, if they were not friends. He was too humane not to hate them. Charles Lamb said with his inimitable sleek pungency that he could read all the books there were; he excluded books that obviously were not books, as cookery books, chessboards bound so as to look like books, and all the works of modern historians and philosophers. One might say in much the same style that Dickens loved all the men in the world; that is he loved all the men whom he was able to recognise as men; the rest he turned into griffins and chimeras without any serious semblance to humanity. Even in his books he never hates a human being. If he wishes to hate him he adopts the simple expedient of making him an inhuman being. Now of these two strands almost the whole of Dickens is made up; they are not only different strands, they are even antagonistic strands. I mean that the whole of Dickens is made up of the strand of satire and the strand of sentimentalism; and the strand of satire is quite unnecessarily merciless and hostile, and the strand of sentimentalism is quite unnecessarily humanitarian and even maudlin. On the proper interweaving of these two things depends the great part of Dickens's success in a novel. And by the consideration of them we can probably best arrive at the solution of the particular emotional enigma of the novel called *Martin Chuzzlewit*.

Martin Chuzzlewit is, I think, vaguely unsatisfactory to the reader, vaguely sad and heavy even to the reader who loves Dickens, because in *Martin Chuzzlewit* more than anywhere else in Dickens's works, more even than in *Oliver Twist*, there is a predominance of the harsh and hostile sort of humour over the hilarious and the humane. It is absurd to lay down any such little rules for the testing of literature. But this may be broadly said and yet with confidence: that Dickens is always at his best when he is laughing at the people whom he really admires. He is at his most humorous in writing of Mr. Pickwick, who represents passive virtue. He is at his most humorous in writing of Mr.

Sam Weller, who represents active virtue. He is never so funny as when he is speaking of people in whom fun itself is a virtue, like the poor people in the Fleet or the Marshalsea. And in the stories that had immediately preceded *Martin Chuzzlewit* he had consistently concerned himself in the majority of cases with the study of such genial and honourable eccentrics; if they are lunatics they are amiable lunatics. In the last important novel before *Martin Chuzzlewit*, *Barnaby Rudge*, the hero himself is an amiable lunatic. In the novel before that, *The Old Curiosity Shop*, the two comic figures, Dick Swiveller and the Marchioness, are not only the most really entertaining, but also the most really sympathetic characters in the book. Before that came *Oliver Twist* (which is, I have said, an exception), and before that *Pickwick*, where the hero is, as Mr. Weller says, "an angel in gaiters." Hitherto, then, on the whole, the central Dickens character had been the man who gave to the poor many things, gold and wine and feasting and good advice; but among other things gave them a good laugh at himself. The jolly old English merchant of the Pickwick type was popular on both counts. People liked to see him throw his money in the gutter. They also liked to see him throw himself there occasionally. In both acts they recognised a common quality of virtue.

Now I think it is certainly the disadvantage of *Martin Chuzzlewit* that none of its absurd characters are thus sympathetic. There are in the book two celebrated characters who are both especially exuberant and amusing even for Dickens, and who are both especially heartless and abominable even for Dickens—

I mean of course Mr. Pecksniff on the one hand and
Mrs. Gamp on the other. The humour of both of
them is gigantesque. Nobody will ever forget the first
time he read the words " Now I should be very glad
to see Mrs. Todgers's idea of a wooden leg." It is
like remembering first love: there is still some sort of
ancient sweetness and sting. I am afraid that, in spite
of many criticisms to the contrary, I am still unable
to take Mr. Pecksniff's hypocrisy seriously. He does
not seem to me so much a hypocrite as a rhetorician;
he reminds me of Serjeant Buzfuz. A very capable
critic, Mr. Noyes, said that I was wrong when I suggested in another place that Dickens must have loved
Pecksniff. Mr. Noyes thinks it clear that Dickens
hated Pecksniff. I cannot believe it. Hatred does
indeed linger round its object as much as love; but
not in that way. Dickens is always making Pecksniff
say things which have a wild poetical truth about
them. Hatred allows no such outbursts of original
innocence. But however that may be the broad fact
remains—Dickens may or may not have loved Pecksniff
comically, but he did not love him seriously; he did not
respect him as he certainly respected Sam Weller.
The same of course is true of Mrs. Gamp. To any one
who appreciates her unctuous and sumptuous conversation it is difficult indeed not to feel that it would
be almost better to be killed by Mrs. Gamp than to be
saved by a better nurse. But the fact remains. In
this book Dickens has not allowed us to love the most
absurd people seriously, and absurd people ought to be
loved seriously. Pecksniff has to be amusing all the
time; the instant he ceases to be laughable he becomes

detestable. Pickwick can take his ease at his inn; he can be leisurely, he can be spacious; he can fall into moods of gravity and even of dulness; he is not bound to be always funny or to forfeit the reader's concern, for he is a good man, and therefore even his dulness is beautiful, just as is the dulness of the animal. We can leave Pickwick a little while by the fire to think; for the thoughts of Pickwick, even if they were to go slowly, would be full of all the things that all men care for— old friends and old inns and memory and the goodness of God. But we dare not leave Pecksniff alone for a moment. We dare not leave him thinking by the fire, for the thoughts of Pecksniff would be too frightful.

CHRISTMAS BOOKS

THE mystery of Christmas is in a manner identical with the mystery of Dickens. If ever we adequately explain the one we may adequately explain the other. And indeed, in the treatment of the two, the chronological or historical order must in some degree be remembered. Before we come to the question of what Dickens did for Christmas we must consider the question of what Christmas did for Dickens. How did it happen that this bustling, nineteenth-century man, full of the almost cock-sure common-sense of the utilitarian and liberal epoch, came to associate his name chiefly in literary history with the perpetuation of a half pagan and half Catholic festival which he would certainly have called an antiquity and might easily have called a superstition? Christmas has indeed been celebrated before in English literature; but it had, in the most noticeable cases, been celebrated in connection with that kind of feudalism with which Dickens would have severed his connection with an ignorant and even excessive scorn. Sir Roger de Coverley kept Christmas; but it was a feudal Christmas. Sir Walter Scott sang in praise of Christmas; but it was a feudal Christmas. And Dickens was not only indifferent to the dignity of the old country gentleman or to the genial archæology of Scott;

he was even harshly and insolently hostile to it.   If
Dickens had lived in the neighbourhood of Sir Roger de
Coverley he would undoubtedly, like Tom Touchy,
have been always "having the law of him."   If
Dickens had stumbled in among the old armour and
quaint folios of Scott's study he would certainly have
read his brother novelist a lesson in no measured terms
about the futility of thus fumbling in the dust-bins of
old oppression and error.   So far from Dickens being
one of those who like a thing because it is old, he was
one of those cruder kind of reformers, in theory at
least, who actually dislike a thing because it is old.
He was not merely the more righteous kind of Radical
who tries to uproot abuses; he was partly also that more
suicidal kind of Radical who tries to uproot himself.   In
theory at any rate, he had no adequate conception of
the importance of human tradition; in his time it had
been twisted and falsified into the form of an opposition
to democracy.   In truth, of course, tradition is the
most democratic of all things, for tradition is merely a
democracy of the dead as well as the living.   But
Dickens and his special group or generation had no
grasp of this permanent position; they had been called
to a special war for the righting of special wrongs.   In
so far as such an institution as Christmas was old,
Dickens would even have tended to despise it.   He
could never have put the matter to himself in the correct
way—that while there are some things whose antiquity
does prove that they are dying, there are some other
things whose antiquity only proves that they cannot
die.   If some Radical contemporary and friend of
Dickens had happened to say to him that in defending

the mince-pies and the mummeries of Christmas he was defending a piece of barbaric and brutal ritualism, doomed to disappear in the light of reason along with the Boy-Bishop and the Lord of Misrule, I am not sure that Dickens (though he was one of the readiest and most rapid masters of reply in history) would have found it very easy upon his own principles to answer. It was by a great ancestral instinct that he defended Christmas; by that sacred sub-consciousness which is called tradition, which some have called a dead thing, but which is really a thing far more living than the intellect. There is a dark kinship and brotherhood of all mankind which is much too deep to be called heredity or to be in any way explained in scientific formulæ; blood is thicker than water and is especially very much thicker than water on the brain. But this unconscious and even automatic quality in Dickens's defence of the Christmas feast, this fact that his defence might almost be called animal rather than mental, though in proper language it should be called merely virile; all this brings us back to the fact that we must begin with the atmosphere of the subject itself. We must not ask Dickens what Christmas is, for with all his heat and eloquence he does not know. Rather we must ask Christmas what Dickens is—ask how this strange child of Christmas came to be born out of due time.

Dickens devoted his genius in a somewhat special sense to the description of happiness. No other literary man of his eminence has made this central human aim so specially his subject matter. Happiness is a mystery —generally a momentary mystery—which seldom stops long enough to submit itself to artistic observation,

and which, even when it is habitual, has something
about it which renders artistic description almost
impossible. There are twenty tiny minor poets who
can describe fairly impressively an eternity of agony;
there are very few even of the eternal poets who can
describe ten minutes of satisfaction. Nevertheless,
mankind being half divine is always in love with the
impossible, and numberless attempts have been made
from the beginning of human literature to describe a
real state of felicity. Upon the whole, I think, the
most successful have been the most frankly physical
and symbolic; the flowers of Eden or the jewels of the
New Jerusalem. Many writers, for instance, have
called the gold and chrysolite of the Holy City a vulgar
lump of jewellery. But when these critics themselves
attempt to describe their conceptions of future happiness, it is always some priggish nonsense about "planes,"
about "cycles of fulfilment," or "spirals of spiritual
evolution." Now a cycle is just as much a physical
metaphor as a flower of Eden; a spiral is just as much
a physical metaphor as a precious stone. But, after
all, a garden is a beautiful thing; whereas this is by
no means necessarily true of a cycle, as can be seen
in the case of a bicycle. A jewel, after all, is a beautiful thing; but this is not necessarily so of a spiral, as
can be seen in the case of a corkscrew. Nothing is
gained by dropping the old material metaphors, which
did hint at heavenly beauty, and adopting other
material metaphors which do not even give a hint of
earthly beauty. This modern or spiral method of
describing indescribable happiness may, I think, be
dismissed. Then there has been another method

which has been adopted by many men of a very real poetical genius. It was the method of the old pastoral poets like Theocritus. It was in another way that adopted by the elegance and piety of Spenser. It was certainly expressed in the pictures of Watteau; and it had a very sympathetic and even manly expression in modern England in the decorative poetry of William Morris. These men of genius, from Theocritus to Morris, occupied themselves in endeavouring to describe happiness as a state of certain human beings, the atmosphere of a commonwealth, the enduring climate of certain cities or islands. They poured forth treasures of the truest kind of imagination upon describing the happy lives and landscapes of Utopia or Atlantis or the Earthly Paradise. They traced with the most tender accuracy the tracery of its fruit-trees or the glimmering garments of its women; they used every ingenuity of colour or intricate shape to suggest its infinite delight. And what they succeeded in suggesting was always its infinite melancholy. William Morris described the Earthly Paradise in such a way that the only strong emotional note left on the mind was the feeling of how homeless his travellers felt in that alien Elysium; and the reader sympathised with them, feeling that he would prefer not only Elizabethan England but even twentieth-century Camberwell to such a land of shining shadows. Thus literature has almost always failed in endeavouring to describe happiness as a state. Human tradition, human custom and folk-lore (though far more true and reliable than literature as a rule) have not often succeeded in giving quite the correct symbols for a real atmosphere of *camaraderie* and joy. But here and there the note has been struck with the sudden vibration of the *vox humana*. In human tradition it has been struck chiefly in the old celebrations of Christmas. In literature it has been struck chiefly in Dickens's Christmas tales.

In the historic celebration of Christmas as it remains from Catholic times in certain northern countries (and it is to be remembered that in Catholic times the northern countries were, if possible, more Catholic than anybody else), there are three qualities which explain, I think, its hold upon the human sense of happiness, especially in such men as Dickens. There are three notes of Christmas, so to speak, which are also notes of happiness, and which the pagans and the Utopians forget. If we state what they are in the case of Christmas, it will be quite sufficiently obvious how important they are in the case of Dickens.

The first quality is what may be called the dramatic quality. The happiness is not a state; it is a crisis. All the old customs surrounding the celebration of the birth of Christ are made by human instinct so as to insist and re-insist upon this crucial quality. Everything is so arranged that the whole household may feel, if possible, as a household does when a child is actually being born in it. The thing is a vigil and a vigil with a definite limit. People sit up at night until they hear the bells ring. Or they try to sleep at night in order to see their presents the next morning. Everywhere there is a limitation, a restraint; at one moment the door is shut, at the moment after it is opened. The hour has come or it has not come; the parcels are undone or they are not undone; there is no evolution of

Christmas presents. This sharp and theatrical quality in pleasure, which human instinct and the mother wit of the world has wisely put into the popular celebrations of Christmas, is also a quality which is essential in such romantic literature as Dickens wrote. In romantic literature the hero and heroine must indeed be happy, but they must also be unexpectedly happy. This is the first connecting link between literature and the old religious feast; this is the first connecting link between Dickens and Christmas.

The second element to be found in all such festivity and all such romance is the element which is represented as well as it could be represented by the mere fact that Christmas occurs in the winter. It is the element not merely of contrast, but actually of antagonism. It preserves everything that was best in the merely primitive or pagan view of such ceremonies or such banquets. If we are carousing, at least we are warriors carousing. We hang above us, as it were, the shields and battle-axes with which we must do battle with the giants of the snow and hail. All comfort must be based on discomfort. Man chooses when he wishes to be most joyful the very moment when the whole material universe is most sad. It is this contradiction and mystical defiance which gives a quality of manliness and reality to the old winter feasts which is not characteristic of the sunny felicities of the Earthly Paradise. And this curious element has been carried out even in all the trivial jokes and tasks that have always surrounded such occasions as these. The object of the jovial customs was not to make everything artificially easy: on the contrary, it was rather to make everything

artificially difficult. Idealism is not only expressed
by shooting an arrow at the stars; the fundamental
principle of idealism is also expressed by putting a leg
of mutton at the top of a greasy pole. There is in all
such observances a quality which can be called only
the quality of divine obstruction. For instance, in
the game of snapdragon (that admirable occupation)
the conception is that raisins taste much nicer if they
are brands saved from the burning. About all Christmas things there is something a little nobler, if only
nobler in form and theory, than mere comfort; even
holly is prickly. It is not hard to see the connection
of this kind of historic instinct with a romantic writer
like Dickens. The healthy novelist must always play
snapdragon with his principal characters; he must
always be snatching the hero and heroine like raisins
out of the fire.

The third great Christmas element is the element
of the grotesque. The grotesque is the natural expression of joy; and all the Utopias and new Edens
of the poets fail to give a real impression of enjoyment,
very largely because they leave out the grotesque. A
man in most modern Utopias cannot really be happy;
he is too dignified. A man in Morris's Earthly Paradise cannot really be enjoying himself; he is too decorative. When real human beings have real delights they
tend to express them entirely in grotesques—I might
almost say entirely in goblins. On Christmas Eve one
may talk about ghosts so long as they are turnip ghosts.
But one would not be allowed (I hope, in any decent
family) to talk on Christmas Eve about astral bodies.
The boar's head of old Yule-time was as grotesque as

the donkey's head of Bottom the Weaver. But there is only one set of goblins quite wild enough to express the wild goodwill of Christmas. Those goblins are the characters of Dickens.

Arcadian poets and Arcadian painters have striven to express happiness by means of beautiful figures. Dickens understood that happiness is best expressed by ugly figures. In beauty, perhaps, there is something allied to sadness; certainly there is something akin to joy in the grotesque, nay, in the uncouth. There is something mysteriously associated with happiness not only in the corpulence of Falstaff and the corpulence of Tony Weller, but even in the red nose of Bardolph or the red nose of Mr. Stiggins. A thing of beauty is an inspiration for ever—a matter of meditation for ever. It is rather a thing of ugliness that is strictly a joy for ever.

All Dickens's books are Christmas books. But this is still truest of his two or three famous Yuletide tales—*The Christmas Carol* and *The Chimes* and *The Cricket on the Hearth*. Of these *The Christmas Carol* is beyond comparison the best as well as the most popular. Indeed, Dickens is in so profound and spiritual a sense a popular author that in his case, unlike most others, it can generally be said that the best work is the most popular. It is for *Pickwick* that he is best known; and upon the whole it is for Pickwick that he is best worth knowing. In any case this superiority of *The Christmas Carol* makes it convenient for us to take it as an example of the generalisations already made. If we study the very real atmosphere of rejoicing and of riotous charity in *The Christmas Carol* we shall find that all the three marks I have mentioned are unmistakably visible. *The Christmas Carol* is a happy story first, because it describes an abrupt and dramatic change. It is not only the story of a conversion, but of a sudden conversion; as sudden as the conversion of a man at a Salvation Army meeting. Popular religion is quite right in insisting on the fact of a crisis in most things. It is true that the man at the Salvation Army meeting would probably be converted from the punch bowl; whereas Scrooge was converted to it. That only means that Scrooge and Dickens represented a higher and more historic Christianity.

Again, *The Christmas Carol* owes much of its hilarity to our second source—the fact of its being a tale of winter and of a very wintry winter. There is much about comfort in the story; yet the comfort is never enervating: it is saved from that by a tingle of something bitter and bracing in the weather. Lastly, the story exemplifies throughout the power of the third principle—the kinship between gaiety and the grotesque. Everybody is happy because nobody is dignified. We have a feeling somehow that Scrooge looked even uglier when he was kind than he had looked when he was cruel. The turkey that Scrooge bought was so fat, says Dickens, that it could never have stood upright. That top-heavy and monstrous bird is a good symbol of the top-heavy happiness of the stories.

It is less profitable to criticise the other two tales in detail because they represent variations on the theme in two directions; and variations that were not, upon the whole, improvements. *The Chimes* is a monument of

Dickens's honourable quality of pugnacity.   He could not admire anything, even peace, without wanting to be warlike about it.   That   was   all   as   it   should be.

DOMBEY AND SON

IN Dickens's literary life *Dombey and Son* represents a break so important as to necessitate our casting back to a summary and a generalisation. In order fully to understand what this break is, we must say something of the previous character of Dickens's novels, and even something of the general character of novels in themselves. How essential this is we shall see shortly.

It must first be remembered that the novel is the most typical of modern forms. It is typical of modern forms especially in this, that it is essentially formless. All the ancient modes or structures of literature were definite and severe. Any one composing them had to abide by their rules; they were what their name implied. Thus a tragedy might be a bad tragedy, but it was always a tragedy. Thus an epic might be a bad epic, but it was always an epic. Now in the sense in which there is such a thing as an epic, in that sense there is no such thing as a novel. We call any long fictitious narrative in prose a novel, just as we call any short piece of prose without any narrative an essay. Both these forms are really quite formless, and both of them are really quite new. The difference between a good epic by Mr. John Milton and a bad epic by Mr. John Smith was simply the difference between the same thing done

well and the same thing done badly. But it was not
(for instance) like the difference between *Clarissa
Harlowe* and *The Time Machine*. If we class Richard-
son's book with Mr. Wells's book it is really only for
convenience; if we say that they are both novels we
shall certainly be puzzled in that case to say what on
earth a novel is. But the note of our age, both for
good and evil, is a highly poetical and largely illogical
faith in liberty. Liberty is not a negation or a piece
of nonsense, as the cheap reactionaries say; it is a
belief in variety and growth. But it is a purely poetic
and even a merely romantic belief. The nineteenth
century was an age of romance as certainly as the
Middle Ages was an age of reason. Mediævals liked
to have everything defined and defensible; the modern
world prefers to run some risks for the sake of spon-
taneity and diversity. Consequently the modern world
is full of a phenomenon peculiar to itself—I mean the
spectacle of small or originally small things swollen to
enormous size and power. The modern world is like
a world in which toadstools should be as big as trees,
and insects should walk about in the sun as large as
elephants. Thus, for instance, the shopkeeper, almost
an unimportant figure in carefully ordered states, has
in our time become the millionaire, and has more power
than ten kings. Thus again a practical knowledge of
nature, of the habits of animals or the properties of
fire and water, was in the old ordered state either an
almost servile labour or a sort of joke; it was left to
old women and gamekeepers and boys who went
birds'-nesting. In our time this commonplace daily
knowledge has swollen into the enormous miracle of

physical size, weighing the stars and talking under the sea.   In short, our age is a sort of splendid jungle in which some of the most towering weeds and blossoms have come from the smallest seed.

And this is, generally speaking, the explanation of the novel.   The novel is not so much the filling up of an artistic plan, however new or fantastic.   It is a thing that has grown from some germ of suggestion, and has often turned out much larger than the author intended. And this, lastly, is the final result of these facts, that the critic can generally trace in a novel what was the original artistic type or shape of thought from which the whole matter started, and he will generally find that this is different in every case.   In one novel he will find that the first impulse is a character.   In another novel he will find that the first impulse is a landscape, the atmosphere of some special countryside. In another novel he will find that the first impulse is the last chapter.   Or it may be a thrust with sword or dagger, it may be a theology, it may be a song.   Somewhere embedded in every ordinary book are the five or six words for which really all the rest will be written. Some of our enterprising editors who set their readers to hunt for banknotes and missing ladies might start a competition for finding those words in every novel. But whether or no this is possible, there is no doubt that the principle in question is of great importance in the case of Dickens, and especially in the case of *Dombey and Son.*

In all the Dickens novels can be seen, so to speak, the original thing that they were before they were novels. The same may be observed, for the matter of that, in

the great novels of most of the great modern novelists.
For example, Sir Walter Scott wrote poetical romances
before he wrote prose romances. Hence it follows
that, with all their much greater merit, his novels
may still be described as poetical romances in prose.
While adding a new and powerful element of popular
humours and observation, Scott still retains a certain
purely poetical right—a right to make his heroes and
outlaws and great kings speak at the great moments
with a rhetoric so rhythmical that it partakes of the
nature of song, the same quite metrical rhetoric which
is used in the metrical speeches of Marmion or Roderick
Dhu. In the same way, although *Don Quixote* is a
modern novel in its irony and subtlety, we can see that
it comes from the old long romances of chivalry. In
the same way, although *Clarissa* is a modern novel in
its intimacy and actuality, we can see that it comes
from the old polite letter-writing and polite essays
of the period of the *Spectator*. Any one can see that
Scott formed in *The Lay of the Last Minstrel* the style
that he applied again and again afterwards, like the
reappearances of a star taking leave of the stage. All
his other romances were positively last appearances of
the positively last Minstrel. Any one can see that
Thackeray formed in fragmentary satires like *The Book
of Snobs* or *The Yellowplush Papers* the style, the rather
fragmentary style, in which he was to write *Vanity Fair*.
In most modern cases, in short (until very lately, at
any rate), the novel is an enormous outgrowth from
something that was not a novel. And in Dickens this
is very important. All his novels are outgrowths of
the original notion of taking notes, splendid and

inspired notes, of what happens in the street. Those in the modern world who cannot reconcile themselves to his method—those who feel that there is about his books something intolerably clumsy or superficial—have either no natural taste for strong literature at all, or else have fallen into their error by too persistently regarding Dickens as a modern novelist and expecting all his books to be modern novels. Dickens did not know at what exact point he really turned into a novelist. Nor do we. Dickens did not know, in his deepest soul, whether he ever really did turn into a novelist. Nor do we. The novel being a modern product is one of the few things to which we really can apply that disgusting method of thought—the method of evolution. But even in evolution there are great gaps, there are great breaks, there are great crises. I have said that the first of these breaks in Dickens may be placed at the point when he wrote *Nicholas Nickleby*. This was his first serious decision to be a novelist in any sense at all, to be anything except a maker of momentary farces. The second break, and that a far more important break, is in *Dombey and Son*. This marks his final resolution to be a novelist and nothing else, to be a serious constructor of fiction in the serious sense. Before *Dombey and Son* even his pathos had been really frivolous. After *Dombey and Son* even his absurdity was intentional and grave.

In case this transition is not understood, one or two tests may be taken at random. The episodes in *Dombey and Son*, the episodes in *David Copperfield*, which came after it, are no longer episodes merely stuck into the middle of the story without any connec-

tion with it, like most of the episodes in *Nicholas
Nickleby*, or most of the episodes even in *Martin
Chuzzlewit*. Take, for instance, by way of a mere
coincidence, the fact that three schools for boys are
described successively in *Nicholas Nickleby*, in *Dombey
and Son*, and in *David Copperfield*. But the difference
is enormous. Dotheboys Hall does not exist to tell us
anything about Nicholas Nickleby. Rather Nicholas
Nickleby exists entirely in order to tell us about Dotheboys Hall. It does not in any way affect his history or
psychology; he enters Mr. Squeers's school and leaves
Mr. Squeers's school with the same character, or rather
absence of character. It is a mere episode, existing
for itself. But when little Paul Dombey goes to an old-
fashioned but kindly school, it is in a very different
sense and for a very different reason from that for
which Nicholas Nickleby goes to an old-fashioned and
cruel school. The sending of little Paul to Dr. Blimber's is a real part of the history of little Paul, such as
it is. Dickens deliberately invents all that elderly
pedantry in order to show up Paul's childishness.
Dickens deliberately invents all that rather heavy
kindness in order to show up Paul's predestination and
tragedy. Dotheboys Hall is not meant to show up
anything except Dotheboys Hall. But although Dickens doubtless enjoyed Dr. Blimber quite as much as Mr.
Squeers, it remains true that Dr. Blimber is really a
very good foil to Paul; whereas Squeers is not a foil to
Nicholas; Nicholas is merely a lame excuse for Squeers.
The change can be seen continued in the school, or
rather the two schools, to which David Copperfield
goes. The whole idea of David Copperfield's life

is that he had the dregs of life before the wine of it.
He knew the worst of the world before he knew the
best of it. His childhood at Dr. Strong's is a second
childhood. Now for this purpose the two schools are
perfectly well adapted. Mr. Creakle's school is not
only, like Mr. Squeers's school, a bad school, it is a bad
influence upon David Copperfield. Dr. Strong's school
is not only a good school, it is a good influence upon
David Copperfield. I have taken this case of the
schools as a case casual but concrete. The same, however, can be seen in any of the groups or incidents of
the novels on both sides of the boundary. Mr. Crummles's theatrical company is only a society that Nicholas happens to fall into. America is only a place to
which Martin Chuzzlewit happens to go. These things
are isolated sketches, and nothing else. Even Todgers's
boarding-house is only a place where Mr. Pecksniff
can be delightfully hypocritical. It is not a place which
throws any new light on Mr. Pecksniff's hypocrisy.
But the case is different with that more subtle hypocrite
in *Dombey and Son*—I mean Major Bagstock. Dickens
does mean it as a deliberate light on Mr. Dombey's
character that he basks with a fatuous calm in the blazing sun of Major Bagstock's tropical and offensive
flattery. Here, then, is the essence of the change. He
not only wishes to write a novel; this he did as early
as *Nicholas Nickleby*. He wishes to have as little as
possible in the novel that does not really assist
it as a novel. Previously he had asked with the
assistance of what incidents could his hero wander
farther and farther from the pathway. Now he
has really begun to ask with the assistance of what

incidents his hero can get nearer and nearer to the goal.

The change made Dickens a greater novelist. I am not sure that it made him a greater man. One good character by Dickens requires all eternity to stretch its legs in; and the characters in his later books are always being tripped up by some tiresome nonsense about the story. For instance, in *Dombey and Son*, Mrs. Skewton is really very funny. But nobody with a love of the real smell of Dickens would compare her for a moment, for instance, with Mrs. Nickleby. And the reason of Mrs. Skewton's inferiority is simply this, that she has something to do in the plot; she has to entrap or assist to entrap Mr. Dombey into marrying Edith. Mrs. Nickleby, on the other hand, has nothing at all to do in the story, except to get in everybody's way. The consequence is that we complain not of her for getting in everyone's way, but of everyone for getting in hers. What are suns and stars, what are times and seasons, what is the mere universe, that it should presume to interrupt Mrs. Nickleby? Mrs. Skewton (though supposed, of course, to be a much viler sort of woman) has something of the same quality of splendid and startling irrelevancy. In her also there is the same feeling of wild threads hung from world to world like the webs of gigantic spiders; of things connected that seem to have no connection save by this one adventurous filament of frail and daring folly. Nothing could be better than Mrs. Skewton when she finds herself, after convolutions of speech, somehow on the subject of Henry VIII., and pauses to mention with approval "his dear little peepy eyes and his benevolent chin."

Nothing could be better than her attempt at Mahome-
dan resignation when she feels almost inclined to say
"that there is no What's-his-name but Thingummy,
and What-you-may-call-it is his prophet!" But she
has not so much time as Mrs. Nickleby to say these
good things; also she has not sufficient human virtue
to say them constantly. She is always intent upon
her worldly plans, among other things upon the worldly
plan of assisting Charles Dickens to get a story finished.
She is always "advancing her shrivelled ear" to listen
to what Dombey is saying to Edith. Worldliness is the
most solemn thing in the world; it is far more solemn
than other-worldliness. Mrs. Nickleby can afford to
ramble as a child does in a field, or as a child does to
laugh at nothing, for she is like a child, innocent. It is
only the good who can afford to be frivolous.

Broadly speaking, what is said here of Mrs. Skewton
applies to the great part of *Dombey and Son*, even to the
comic part of it. It shows an advance in art and unity;
it does not show an advance in genius and creation.
In some cases, in fact, I cannot help feeling that it
shows a falling off. It may be a personal idiosyncrasy,
but there is only one comic character really prominent
in Dickens, upon whom Dickens has really lavished
the wealth of his invention, and who does not amuse
me at all, and that character is Captain Cuttle. But
three great exceptions must be made to any such dis-
paragement of *Dombey and Son*. They are all three
of that royal order in Dickens's creation which can no
more be described or criticised than strong wine. The
first is Major Bagstock, the second is Cousin Feenix,
the third is Toots. In Bagstock Dickens has blasted

for ever that type which pretends to be sincere by the simple operation of being explosively obvious. He tells about a quarter of the truth, and then poses as truthful because a quarter of the truth is much simpler than the whole of it. He is the kind of man who goes about with posers for Bishops or for Socialists, with plain questions to which he wants a plain answer. His questions are plain only in the same sense that he himself is plain—in the sense of being uncommonly ugly. He is the man who always bursts with satisfaction because he can call a spade a spade, as if there were any kind of logical or philosophical use in merely saying the same word twice over. He is the man who wants things down in black and white, as if black and white were the only two colours; as if blue and green and red and gold were not facts of the universe. He is too selfish to tell the truth and too impatient even to hear it. He cannot endure the truth, because it is subtle. This man is almost always like Bagstock—a sycophant and a toad-eater. A man is not any the less a toad-eater because he eats his toads with a huge appetite and gobbles them up, as Bagstock did his breakfast, with the eyes starting out of his purple face. He flatters brutally. He cringes with a swagger. And men of the world like Dombey are always taken in by him, because men of the world are probably the simplest of all the children of Adam.

Cousin Feenix again is an exquisite suggestion, with his rickety chivalry and rambling compliments. It was about the period of *Dombey and Son* that Dickens began to be taken up by good society. (One can use only vulgar terms for an essentially vulgar process.)

And his sketches of the man of good family in the books of this period show that he had had glimpses of what that singular world is like. The aristocrats in his earliest books are simply dragons and griffins for his heroes to fight with—monsters like Sir Mulberry Hawk or Lord Verisopht. They are merely created upon the old principle, that your scoundrel must be polite and powerful—a very sound principle. The villain must be not only a villain, but a tyrant. The giant must be larger than Jack. But in the books of the Dombey period we have many shrewd glimpses of the queer realities of English aristocracy. Of these Cousin Feenix is one of the best. Cousin Feenix is a much better sketch of the essentially decent and chivalrous aristocrat than Sir Leicester Dedlock. Both of the men are, if you will, fools, as both are honourable gentlemen. But if one may attempt a classification among fools, Sir Leicester Dedlock is a stupid fool, while Cousin Feenix is a silly fool—which is much better. The difference is that the silly fool has a folly which is always on the borderland of wit, and even of wisdom; his wandering wits come often upon undiscovered truths. The stupid fool is as consistent and as homogeneous as wood; he is as invincible as the ancestral darkness. Cousin Feenix is a good sketch of the sort of well-bred old ass who is so fundamentally genuine that he is always saying very true things by accident. His whole tone also, though exaggerated like everything in Dickens, is very true to the bewildered good nature which marks English aristocratic life. The statement that Dickens could not describe a gentleman is, like most popular animadversions against

Dickens, so very thin and one-sided a truth as to be for serious purposes a falsehood. When people say that Dickens could not describe a gentleman, what they mean is this, and so far what they mean is true. They mean that Dickens could not describe a gentleman as gentlemen feel a gentleman. They mean that he could not take that atmosphere easily, accept it as the normal atmosphere, or describe that world from the inside. This is true. In Dickens's time there was such a thing as the English people, and Dickens belonged to it. Because there is no such thing as an English people now, almost all literary men drift towards what is called Society; almost all literary men either are gentlemen or pretend to be. Hence, as I say, when we talk of describing a gentleman, we always mean describing a gentleman from the point of view of one who either belongs to, or is interested in perpetuating, that type. Dickens did not describe gentlemen in the way that gentlemen describe gentlemen. He described them in the way in which he described waiters, or railway guards, or men drawing with chalk on the pavement. He described them, in short (and this we may freely concede), from the outside, as he described any other oddity or special trade. But when it comes to saying that he did not describe them well, then that is quite another matter, and that I should emphatically deny. The things that are really odd about the English upper class he saw with startling promptitude and penetration, and if the English upper class does not see these odd things in itself, it is not because they are not there, but because we are all blind to our own oddities; it is for the same reason that tramps do not feel dirty, or that niggers do not feel black. I have often heard a dear old English oligarch say that Dickens could not describe a gentleman, while every note of his own voice and turn of his own hand recalled Sir Leicester Dedlock. I have often been told by some old buck that Dickens could not describe a gentleman, and been told so in the shaky voice and with all the vague allusiveness of Cousin Feenix.

Cousin Feenix has really many of the main points of the class that governs England. Take, for an instance, his hazy notion that he is in a world where everybody knows everybody; whenever he mentions a man, it is a man "with whom my friend Dombey is no doubt acquainted." That pierces to the very helpless soul of aristocracy. Take again the stupendous gravity with which he leads up to a joke. That is the very soul of the House of Commons and the Cabinet, of the high-class English politics, where a joke is always enjoyed solemnly. Take his insistence upon the technique of Parliament, his regrets for the time when the rules of debate were perhaps better observed than they are now. Take that wonderful mixture in him (which is the real human virtue of our aristocracy) of a fair amount of personal modesty with an innocent assumption of rank. Of a man who saw all these genteel foibles so clearly it is absurd merely to say without further explanation that he could not describe a gentleman. Let us confine ourselves to saying that he did not describe a gentleman as gentlemen like to be described.

Lastly, there is the admirable study of Toots, who may be considered as being in some ways the masterpiece of Dickens. Nowhere else did Dickens express with such astonishing insight and truth his main contention, which is that to be good and idiotic is not a poor fate, but, on the contrary, an experience of primeval innocence, which wonders at all things. Dickens did not know, any more than any great man ever knows, what was the particular thing that he had to preach. He did not know it; he only preached it. But the particular thing that he had to preach was this: That humility is the only possible basis of enjoyment; that if one has no other way of being humble except being poor, then it is better to be poor, and to enjoy; that if one has no other way of being humble except being imbecile, then it is better to be imbecile, and to enjoy. That is the deep unconscious truth in the character of Toots—that all his externals are flashy and false; all his internals unconscious, obscure, and true. He wears loud clothes, and he is silent inside them. His shirts and waistcoats are covered with bright spots of pink and purple, while his soul is always covered with the sacred shame. He always gets all the outside things of life wrong, and all the inside things right. He always admires the right Christian people, and gives them the wrong Christian names. Dimly connecting Captain Cuttle with the shop of Mr. Solomon Gills, he always addresses the astonished mariner as "Captain Gills."   He turns Mr. Walter Gay, by a most improving transformation, into "Lieutenant Walters." But he always knows which people upon his own principles to admire. He forgets who they are, but he remembers what they are. With the clear eyes of humility he perceives the whole world as it is.

He respects the Game Chicken for being strong, as even the Game Chicken ought to be respected for being strong. He respects Florence for being good, as even Florence ought to be respected for being good. And he has no doubt about which he admires most; he prefers goodness to strength, as do all masculine men. It is through the eyes of such characters as Toots that Dickens really sees the whole of his tales. For even if one calls him a half-wit, it still makes a difference that he keeps the right half of his wits. When we think of the unclean and craven spirit in which Toots might be treated in a psychological novel of to-day; how he might walk with a mooncalf face, and a brain of bestial darkness, the soul rises in real homage to Dickens for showing how much simple gratitude and happiness can remain in the lopped roots of the most simplified intelligence. If scientists must treat a man as a dog, it need not be always as a mad dog. They might grant him, like Toots, a little of the dog's loyalty and the dog's reward.

DAVID COPPERFIELD

In this book Dickens is really trying to write a new kind of book, and the enterprise is almost as chivalrous as a cavalry charge. He is making a romantic attempt to be realistic. That is almost the definition of *David Copperfield*. In his last book, *Dombey and Son*, we see a certain maturity and even a certain mild exhaustion in his earlier farcical method. He never failed to have fine things in any of his books, and Toots is a very fine thing. Still, I could never find Captain Cuttle and Mr. Sol Gills very funny, and the whole Wooden Midshipman seems to me very wooden. In *David Copperfield* he suddenly unseals a new torrent of truth, the truth out of his own life. The impulse of the thing is autobiography; he is trying to tell all the absurd things that have happened to himself, and not the least absurd thing is himself. Yet though it is Dickens's ablest and clearest book, there is in it a falling away of a somewhat singular kind.

Generally speaking there was astonishingly little of fatigue in Dickens's books. He sometimes wrote bad work; he sometimes wrote even unimportant work; but he wrote hardly a line which is not full of his own fierce vitality and fancy. If he is dull it is hardly ever because he cannot think of anything; it is because, by some silly excitement or momentary lapse of judgment, he has thought of something that was not worth thinking of.   If his joke is feeble, it is as an impromptu joke at an uproarious dinner-table may be feeble; it is no indication of any lack of vitality.   The joke is feeble, but it is not a sign of feebleness.   Broadly speaking, this is true of Dickens.   If his writing is not amusing us, at least it is amusing him.   Even when he is tiring he is not tired.

But in the case of *David Copperfield* there is a real reason for noting an air of fatigue.   For although this is the best of all Dickens's books, it constantly disappoints the critical and intelligent reader.   The reason is that Dickens began it under his sudden emotional impulse of telling the whole truth about himself and gradually allowed the whole truth to be more and more diluted, until towards the end of the book we are back in the old pedantic and decorative art of Dickens, an art which we justly admired in its own place and on its own terms, but which we resent when we feel it gradually returning through a tale pitched originally in a more practical and piercing key.   Here, I say, is the one real example of the fatigue of Dickens.   He begins his story in a new style and then slips back into an old one. The earlier part is in his later manner.   The later part is in his earlier manner.

There are many marks of something weak and shadowy in the end of *David Copperfield*.   Here, for instance, is one of them which is not without its bearing on many tendencies of modern England.   Why did Dickens at the end of this book give way to that typically English optimism about emigration?   He seems to think that he can cure the souls of a whole

cartload, or rather boatload, of his characters by sending them all to the Colonies. Peggotty is a desolate and
insulted parent whose house has been desecrated and his
pride laid low; therefore let him go to Australia. Emily
is a woman whose heart is broken and whose honour is
blasted; but she will be quite happy if she goes to
Australia. Mr. Micawber is a man whose soul cannot
be made to understand the tyranny of time or the limits
of human hope; but he will understand all these things
if he goes to Australia. For it must be noted that
Dickens does not use this emigration merely as a mode
of exit. He does not send these characters away on a
ship merely as a symbol suggesting that they pass
wholly out of his hearer's life. He does definitely
suggest that Australia is a sort of island Valley of
Avalon, where the soul may heal it of its grievous
wound. It is seriously suggested that Peggotty finds
peace in Australia. It is really indicated that Emily
regains her dignity in Australia. It is positively
explained of Mr. Micawber not that he was happy in
Australia (for he would be that anywhere), but that
he was definitely prosperous and practically successful
in Australia; and that he would certainly be nowhere.
Colonising is not talked of merely as a coarse, economic
expedient for going to a new market. It is really
offered as something that will cure the hopeless tragedy
of Peggotty; as something that will cure the still more
hopeless comedy of Micawber.

I will not dwell here on the subsequent adventures
of this very sentimental and extremely English illusion.
It would be an exaggeration to say that Dickens in
this matter is something of a forerunner of much

modern imperialism.   His political views were such
that he would have regarded modern imperialism with
horror and contempt.   Nevertheless there is here something of that hazy sentimentalism which makes some
Imperialists prefer to talk of the fringe of the empire
of which they know nothing, rather than of the heart
of the empire which they know is diseased.   It is
said that in the twilight and decline of Rome, close to
the dark ages, the people in Gaul believed that Britain
was a land of ghosts (perhaps it was foggy), and that
the dead were ferried across to it from the northern
coast of France.   If (as is not entirely impossible) our
own century appears to future ages as a time of temporary decay and twilight, it may be said that there
was attached to England a blessed island called Australia to which the souls of the socially dead were
ferried across to remain in bliss for ever.

This element which is represented by the colonial
optimism at the end of *David Copperfield* is a moral
element.   The truth is that there is something a little
mean about this sort of optimism.   I do not like the
notion of David Copperfield sitting down comfortably
to his tea-table with Agnes, having got rid of all the
inconvenient or distressing characters of the story by
sending them to the other side of the world.   The whole
thing has too much about it of the selfishness of a
family which sends a scapegrace to the Colonies to
starve with its blessing.   There is too much in the
whole thing of that element which was satirised by
an ironic interpretation of the epitaph "Peace, perfect
peace, with loved ones far away."   We should have
thought more of David Copperfield (and also of Charles

Dickens) if he had endeavoured for the rest of his life,
by conversation and comfort, to bind up the wounds
of his old friends from the seaside. We should have
thought more of David Copperfield (and also of Charles
Dickens) if he had faced the possibility of going on till
his dying day lending money to Mr. Wilkins Micawber.
We should have thought more of David Copperfield
(and also of Charles Dickens) if he had not looked upon
the marriage with Dora merely as a flirtation, an
episode which he survived and ought to survive. And
yet the truth is that there is nowhere in fiction where
we feel so keenly the primary human instinct and
principle that a marriage is a marriage and irrevocable,
that such things do leave a wound and also a bond as
in this case of David's short connection with his silly
little wife. When all is said and done, when Dickens
has done his best and his worst, when he has sentimen-
talised for pages and tried to tie up everything in the
pink tape of optimism, the fact, in the psychology of
the reader, still remains. The reader does still feel
that David's marriage to Dora was a real marriage;
and that his marriage to Agnes was nothing, a middle-
aged compromise, a taking of the second best, a sort
of spiritualised and sublimated marriage of convenience.
For all the readers of Dickens Dora is thoroughly
avenged. The modern world (intent on anarchy in
everything, even in Government) refuses to perceive
the permanent element of tragic constancy which in-
heres in all passion, and which is the origin of marriage.
Marriage rests upon the fact that you cannot have your
cake and eat it; that you cannot lose your heart and
have it. But, as I have said, there is perhaps no place

in literature where we feel more vividly the sense of this monogamous instinct in man than in David Copperfield. A man is monogamous even if he is only monogamous for a month; love is eternal even if it is only eternal for a month. It always leaves behind it the sense of something broken and betrayed.

But I have mentioned Dora in this connection only because she illustrates the same fact which Micawber illustrates; the fact that there is at the end of this book too much tendency to bless people and get rid of them. Micawber is a nuisance. Dickens the despot condemns him to exile. Dora is a nuisance. Dickens the despot condemns her to death. But it is the whole business of Dickens in the world to express the fact that such people are the spice and interest of life. It is the whole point of Dickens that there is nobody more worth living with than a strong, splendid, entertaining, immortal nuisance. Micawber interrupts practical life; but what is practical life that it should venture to interrupt Micawber? Dora confuses the housekeeping; but we are not angry with Dora because she confuses the housekeeping. We are angry with the housekeeping because it confuses Dora. I repeat, and it cannot be too much repeated that the whole lesson of Dickens is here. It is better to know Micawber than not to know the minor worries that arise out of knowing Micawber. It is better to have a bad debt and a good friend. In the same way it is better to marry a human and healthy personality which happens to attract you than to marry a mere housewife; for a mere housewife is a mere housekeeper. All this was what Dickens stood for; that the very people who are most

irritating in small business circumstances are often the
people who are most delightful in long stretches of
experience of life. It is just the man who is maddening
when he is ordering a cutlet or arranging an appoint-
ment who is probably the man in whose company it is
worth while to journey steadily towards the grave.
Distribute the dignified people and the capable people
and the highly business-like people among all the
situations which their ambition or their innate corruption may demand; but keep close to your heart,
keep deep in your inner councils the absurd people.
Let the clever people pretend to govern you, let the
unimpeachable people pretend to advise you, but let
the fools alone influence you; let the laughable people
whose faults you see and understand be the only
people who are really inside your life, who really come
near you or accompany you on your lonely march
towards the last impossibility. That is the whole
meaning of Dickens; that we should keep the absurd
people for our friends. And here at the end of *David
Copperfield* he seems in some dim way to deny it. He
seems to want to get rid of the preposterous people
simply because they will always continue to be preposterous. I have a horrible feeling that David Copperfield
will send even his aunt to Australia if she worries him
too much about donkeys.

I repeat, then, that this wrong ending of *David
Copperfield* is one of the very few examples in Dickens
of a real symptom of fatigue. Having created splendid
beings for whom alone life might be worth living,
he cannot endure the thought of his hero living with
them. Having given his hero superb and terrible

friends, he is afraid of the awful and tempestuous vista of their friendship. He slips back into a more superficial kind of story and ends it in a more superficial way. He is afraid of the things he has made; of that terrible figure Micawber; of that yet more terrible figure Dora. He cannot make up his mind to see his hero perpetually entangled in the splendid tortures and sacred surprises that come from living with really individual and unmanageable people. He cannot endure the idea that his fairy prince will not have henceforward a perfectly peaceful time. But the wise old fairy tales (which are the wisest things in the world, at any rate the wisest things of worldly origin), the wise old fairy tales never were so silly as to say that the prince and the princess lived peacefully ever afterwards. The fairy tales said that the prince and princess lived happily ever afterwards: and so they did. They lived happily, although it is very likely that from time to time they threw the furniture at each other. Most marriages, I think, are happy marriages; but there is no such thing as a contented marriage. The whole pleasure of marriage is that it is a perpetual crisis. David Copperfield and Dora quarrelled over the cold mutton; and if they had gone on quarrelling to the end of their lives, they would have gone on loving each other to the end of their lives; it would have been a human marriage. But David Copperfield and Agnes would agree about the cold mutton. And that cold mutton would be very cold.

I have here endeavoured to suggest some of the main merits of Dickens within the framework of one of his faults. I have said that *David Copperfield* represents a rather sad transition from his strongest method to his weakest. Nobody would ever complain of Charles Dickens going on writing his own kind of novels, his old kind of novels. If there be anywhere a man who loves good books, that man wishes that there were four *Oliver Twists* and at least forty-four *Pickwicks*. If there be any one who loves laughter and creation, he would be glad to read a hundred of *Nicholas Nickleby* and two hundred of *The Old Curiosity Shop*. But while any one would have welcomed one of Dickens's own ordered and conventional novels, it was not in this spirit that they welcomed *David Copperfield*.

David Copperfield begins as if it were going to be a new kind of Dickens novel; then it gradually turns into an old kind of Dickens novel. It is here that many readers of this splendid book have been subtly and secretly irritated. Nicholas Nickleby is all very well; we accept him as something which is required to tie the whole affair together. Nicholas is a sort of string or clothes-line on which are hung the limp figure of Smike, the jumping-jack of Mr. Squeers and the twin dolls named Cheeryble. If we do not accept Nicholas Nickleby as the hero of the story, at least we accept him as the title of the story. But in *David Copperfield* Dickens begins something which looks for the moment fresh and startling. In the earlier chapters (the amazing earlier chapters of this book) he does seem to be going to tell the living truth about a living boy and man. It is melancholy to see that sudden fire fading. It is sad to see David Copperfield gradually turning into Nicholas Nickleby. Nicholas Nickleby does not exist at all; he is a quite colourless primary condition of the story. We look through Nicholas Nickleby at the

story just as we look through a plain pane of glass at the
street.   But David Copperfield does begin by existing;
it is only gradually that he gives up that exhausting
habit.

Any fair critical account of Dickens must always
make him out much smaller than he is.   For any fair
criticism of Dickens must take account of his evident
errors, as I have taken account of one of the most
evident of them during the last two or three pages.
It would not even be loyal to conceal them.   But no
honest criticism, no criticism, though it spoke with
the tongues of men and angels, could ever really talk
about Dickens.   In all this that I have said I have not
been talking about Dickens at all.   I say it with equa-
nimity; I say it even with arrogance.   I have been talking about the gaps of Dickens.   I have been talking
about the omissions of Dickens.   I have been talking
about the slumber of Dickens and the forgetfulness and
unconsciousness of Dickens.   In one word, I have been
talking not about Dickens, but about the absence of
Dickens.   But when we come to him and his work
itself, what is there to be said?   What is there to be
said about earthquake and the dawn?   He has created,
especially in this book of *David Copperfield*, he has
created, creatures who cling to us and tyrannise over
us, creatures whom we would not forget if we could,
creatures whom we could not forget if we would,
creatures who are more actual than the man who
made them.

This is the excuse for all that indeterminate and rambling and sometimes sentimental criticism of which
Dickens, more than any one else, is the victim, of

which I fear that I for one have made him the victim in
this place.   When I was a boy I could not understand why the Dickensians worried so wearily about
Dickens, about where he went to school and where he
ate his dinners, about how he wore his trousers and
when he cut his hair.   I used to wonder why they did
not write something that I could read about a man like
Micawber.   But I have come to the conclusion that
this almost hysterical worship of the man, combined
with a comparatively feeble criticism on his works,
is just and natural.   Dickens was a man like ourselves;
we can see where he went wrong, and study him without
being stunned or getting the sunstroke.   But Micawber
is not a man; Micawber is the superman.   We can
only walk round and round him wondering what we
shall say.   All the critics of Dickens, when all is said
and done, have only walked round and round Micawber
wondering what they should say.   I am myself at
this moment walking round and round Micawber
wondering what I shall say.   And I have not found out
yet.

CHRISTMAS STORIES

THE power of Dickens is shown even in the scraps of Dickens, just as the virtue of a saint is said to be shown in fragments of his property or rags from his robe. It is with such fragments that we are chiefly concerned in the *Christmas Stories*. Many of them are fragments in the literal sense; Dickens began them and then allowed some one else to carry them on; they are almost rejected notes. In all the other cases we have been considering the books that he wrote; here we have rather to consider the books that he might have written. And here we find the final evidence and the unconscious stamp of greatness, as we might find it in some broken bust or some rejected moulding in the studio of Michael Angelo.

These sketches or parts of sketches all belong to that period in his later life when he had undertaken the duties of an editor, the very heavy duties of a very popular editor. He was not by any means naturally fitted for that position. He was the best man in the world for founding papers; but many people wished that he could have been buried under the foundations, like the first builder in some pagan and prehistoric pile. He called the *Daily News* into existence, but when once it existed, it objected to him strongly. It is not easy,

and perhaps it is not important, to state truly the
cause of this incapacity. It was not in the least what
is called the ordinary fault or weakness of the artist.
It was not that he was careless; rather it was that he
was too conscientious. It was not that he had the
irresponsibility of genius; rather it was that he had the
irritating responsibility of genius; he wanted everybody to see things as he saw them. But in spite of
all this he certainly ran two great popular periodicals—
Household Words and *All the Year Round*—with enormous popular success. And he certainly so far succeeded
in throwing himself into the communism of journalism,
into the nameless brotherhood of a big paper, that many
earnest Dickensians are still engaged in picking out
pieces of Dickens from the anonymous pages of *Household Words* and *All the Year Round*, and those parts
which have been already beyond question picked
out and proved are often fragmentary. The genuine
writing of Dickens breaks off at a certain point, and the
writing of some one else begins. But when the writing
of Dickens breaks off, I fancy that we know it.

The singular thing is that some of the best work that
Dickens ever did, better than the work in his best
novels, can be found in these slight and composite
scraps of journalism. For instance, the solemn and
self-satisfied account of the duty and dignity of a
waiter given in the opening chapter of *Somebody's
Luggage* is quite as full and fine as anything done anywhere by its author in the same vein of sumptuous
satire. It is as good as the account which Mr. Bumble
gives of out-door relief, which, "properly understood,
is the parochial safeguard. The great thing is to give

the paupers what they don't want, and then they never come again." It is as good as Mr. Podsnap's description of the British Constitution, which was bestowed on him by Providence. None of these celebrated passages is more obviously Dickens at his best than this, the admirable description of "the true principles of waitering," or the account of how the waiter's father came back to his mother in broad daylight, "in itself an act of madness on the part of a waiter," and how he expired repeating continually "two and six is three and four is nine." That waiter's explanatory soliloquy might easily have opened an excellent novel, as *Martin Chuzzlewit* is opened by the clever nonsense about the genealogy of the Chuzzlewits, or as *Bleak House* is opened by a satiric account of the damp, dim life of a law court. Yet Dickens practically abandoned the scheme of *Somebody's Luggage;* he only wrote two sketches out of those obviously intended. He may almost be said to have only written a brilliant introduction to another man's book.

Yet it is exactly in such broken outbreaks that his greatness appears. If a man has flung away bad ideas he has shown his sense, but if he has flung away good ideas he has shown his genius. He has proved that he actually has that over-pressure of pure creativeness which we see in nature itself, "that of a hundred seeds, she often brings but one to bear." Dickens had to be Malthusian about his spiritual children. Critics have called Keats and others who died young "the great Might-have-beens of literary history." Dickens certainly was not merely a great Might-have-been. Dickens, to say the least of him, was a great Was.

Yet this fails fully to express the richness of his talent; for the truth is that he was a great Was and also a great Might-have-been. He said what he had to say, and yet not all he had to say. Wild pictures, possible stories, tantalising and attractive trains of thought, perspectives of adventure, crowded so continually upon his mind that at the end there was a vast mass of them left over, ideas that he literally had not the opportunity to develop, tales that he literally had not the time to tell. This is shown clearly in his private notes and letters, which are full of schemes singularly striking and suggestive, schemes which he never carried out. It is indicated even more clearly by these *Christmas Stories*, collected out of the chaotic opulence of *Household Words* and *All the Year Round*. He wrote short stories actually because he had not time to write long stories. He often put into the short story a deep and branching idea which would have done very well for a long story; many of his long stories, so to speak, broke off short. This is where he differs from most who are called the Might-have-beens of literature. Marlowe and Chatterton failed because of their weakness. Dickens failed because of his force.

Examine for example this case of the waiter in *Somebody's Luggage*. Dickens obviously knew enough about that waiter to have made him a running spring of joy throughout a whole novel; as the beadle is in *Oliver Twist*, or the undertaker in *Martin Chuzzlewit*. Every touch of him tingles with truth, from the vague gallantry with which he asks, "Would'st thou know, fair reader (if of the adorable female sex)" to the official severity with which he takes the chambermaid down, "as many pegs as is desirable for the future comfort of all parties." If Dickens had developed this character at full length in a book he would have preserved for ever in literature a type of great humour and great value, and a type which may only too soon be disappearing from English history. He would have eternalised the English waiter. He still exists in some sound old taverns and decent country inns, but there is no one left really capable of singing his praises. I know that Mr. Bernard Shaw has done something of the sort in the delightfully whimsical account of William in *You Never Can Tell.* But nothing will persuade me that Mr. Bernard Shaw can really understand the English waiter. He can never have ordered wine from him for instance. And though the English waiter is by the nature of things solemn about everything, he can never reach the true height and ecstasy of his solemnity except about wine. What the real English waiter would do or say if Mr. Shaw asked him for a vegetarian meal I cannot dare to predict. I rather think that for the first time in his life he would laugh— a horrible sight.

Dickens's waiter is described by one who is not merely witty, truthful, and observant, like Mr. Bernard Shaw, but one who really knew the atmosphere of inns, one who knew and even liked the smell of beef, and beer, and brandy. Hence there is a richness in Dickens's portrait which does not exist in Mr. Shaw's. Mr. Shaw's waiter is merely a man of tact; Dickens's is a man of principle. Mr. Shaw's waiter is an opportunist, just as Mr. Shaw is an opportunist in politics. Dickens's waiter is ready to stand up seriously for "the true principles of waitering," just as Dickens was ready to stand up for the true principles of Liberalism. Mr. Shaw's waiter is agnostic; his motto is "You never can tell." Dickens's waiter is a dogmatist; his motto is "You can tell; I will tell you." And the true old-fashioned English waiter had really this grave and even moral attitude; he was the servant of the customers as a priest is the servant of the faithful, but scarcely in any less dignified sense. Surely it is not mere patriotic partiality that makes one lament the disappearance of this careful and honourable figure crowded out by meaner men at meaner wages, by the German waiter who has learnt five languages in the course of running away from his own, or the Italian waiter who regards those he serves with a darkling contempt which must certainly be that either of a dynamiter or an exiled prince. The human and hospitable English waiter is vanishing. And Dickens might perhaps have saved him, as he saved Christmas.

I have taken this case of the waiter in Dickens and his equally important counterpart in England as an example of the sincere and genial sketches scattered about these short stories. But there are many others, and one at least demands special mention; I mean Mrs. Lirriper, the London landlady. Not only did Dickens never do anything better in a literary sense, but he never performed more perfectly his main moral function, that of insisting through laughter and flippancy upon the virtue of Christian charity. There has been much broad farce against the lodging-house keeper: he alone could have written broad farce in her favour. It is fashionable to represent the landlady as a tyrant;

it is too much forgotten that if she is one of the oppressors she is at least as much one of the oppressed. If she is bad-tempered it is often for the same reasons that make all women bad-tempered (I suppose the exasperating qualities of the other sex); if she is grasping it is often because when a husband makes generosity a vice it is often necessary that a wife should make avarice a virtue. All this Dickens suggested very soundly and in a few strokes in the more remote character of Miss Wozenham. But in Mrs. Lirriper he went further and did not fare worse. In Mrs. Lirriper he suggested quite truly how huge a mass of real good humour, of grand unconscious patience, of unfailing courtesy and constant and difficult benevolence is concealed behind many a lodging-house door and compact in the red-faced person of many a preposterous landlady. Any one could easily excuse the ill-humour of the poor. But great masses of the poor have not even any ill-humour to be excused. Their cheeriness is startling enough to be the foundation of a miracle play; and certainly is startling enough to be the foundation of a romance. Yet I do not know of any romance in which it is expressed except this one.

Of the landlady as of the waiter it may be said that Dickens left in a slight sketch what he might have developed through a long and strong novel. For Dickens had hold of one great truth, the neglect of which has, as it were, truncated and made meagre the work of many brilliant modern novelists. Modern novelists try to make long novels out of subtle characters. But a subtle character soon comes to an end, because it works in and in to its own centre and dies there. But a

simple character goes on for ever in a fresh interest
and energy, because it works out and out into the
infinite universe. Mr. George Moore in France is not
by any means so interesting as Mrs. Lirriper in France;
for she is trying to find France and he is only trying
to find George Moore. Mrs. Lirriper is the female
equivalent of Mr. Pickwick. Unlike Mrs. Bardell
(another and lesser landlady) she was fully worthy to
be Mrs. Pickwick. For in both cases the essential
truth is the same; that original innocence which alone
deserves adventures and because it alone can appreciate
them. We have had Mr. Pickwick in England and
we can imagine him in France. We have had Mrs.
Lirriper in France and we can imagine her in Mesopo-
tamia or in heaven. The subtle character in the
modern novels we cannot really imagine anywhere
except in the suburbs or in Limbo.

BLEAK HOUSE

Bleak House is not certainly Dickens's best book; but
perhaps it is his best novel. Such a distinction is not
a mere verbal trick; it has to be remembered rather
constantly in connection with his work. This particular story represents the highest point of his intellectual maturity. Maturity does not necessarily mean
perfection. It is idle to say that a mature potato is
perfect; some people like new potatoes. A mature
potato is not perfect, but it is a mature potato; the
mind of an intelligent epicure may find it less adapted to
his particular purpose; but the mind of an intelligent
potato would at once admit it as being, beyond all
doubt, a genuine, fully developed specimen of his own
particular species. The same is in some degree true
even of literature. We can say more or less when a
human being has come to his full mental growth, even
if we go so far as to wish that he had never come to it.
Children are very much nicer than grown-up people;
but there is such a thing as growing up. When Dickens wrote *Bleak House* he had grown up.

Like Napoleon, he had made his army on the march.
He had walked in front of his mob of aggressive characters as Napoleon did in front of the half-baked
battalions of the Revolution. And, like Napoleon, he
won battle after battle before he knew his own plan

of campaign; like Napoleon, he put the enemies' forces
to rout before he had put his own force into order   Like
Napoleon, he had a victorious army almost before he
had an army. After his decisive victories Napoleon
began to put his house in order; after his decisive
victories Dickens also began to put his house in order.
The house, when he had put it in order, was *Bleak House.*

There was one thing common to nearly all the other
Dickens tales, with the possible exception of *Dombey
and Son.* They were all rambling tales; and they all
had a perfect right to be. They were all rambling
tales for the very simple reason that they were all about
rambling people. They were novels of adventure;
they were even diaries of travel.   Since the hero strayed
from place to place, it did not seem unreasonable that
the story should stray from subject to subject.   This is
true of the bulk of the novels up to and including *David
Copperfield,* up to the very brink or threshold of *Bleak
House.*   Mr. Pickwick wanders about on the white
English roads, always looking for antiquities and always finding novelties.   Poor Oliver Twist wanders
along the same white roads to seek his fortune and to
find his misfortune.   Nicholas Nickleby goes walking
across England because he is young and hopeful;
Little Nell's grandfather does the same thing because
he is old and silly.   There is not much in common between Samuel Pickwick and Oliver Twist; there is not
much in common between Oliver Twist and Nicholas
Nickleby; there is not much in common (let us hope)
between Little Nell's grandfather and any other human
being.   But they all have this in common, that they
may actually all have trodden in each other's footprints.

They were all wanderers on the face of the same fair English land. *Martin Chuzzlewit* was only made popular by the travels of the hero in America. When we come to *Dombey and Son* we find, as I have said, an exception; but even here it is odd to note the fact that it was an exception almost by accident. In Dickens's original scheme of the story, much greater prominence was to have been given to the travels and trials of Walter Gay; in fact, the young man was to have had a deterioration of character which could only have been adequately detailed in him in his character of a vagabond and a wastrel. The most important point, however, is that when we come to *David Copperfield*, in some sense the summit of his serious literature, we find the thing still there. The hero still wanders from place to place, his genius is still gipsy. The adventures in the book are less violent and less improbable than those which wait for Pickwick and Nicholas Nickleby; but they are still adventures and not merely events; they are still things met on a road. The facts of the story fall away from David as such facts do fall away from a traveller walking fast. We are more likely perhaps, to pass by Mr. Creakle's school than to pass by Mrs. Jarley's wax-works. The only point is that we should pass by both of them. Up to this point in Dickens's development, his novel, however true, is still picaresque; his hero never really rests anywhere in the story. No one seems really to know where Mr. Pickwick lived. Here he has no abiding city.

When we come to *Bleak House*, we come to a change in artistic structure. The thing is no longer a string of incidents; it is a cycle of incidents. It returns upon

itself; it has recurrent melody and poetic justice; it
has artistic constancy and artistic revenge. It preserves
the unities; even to some extent it preserves the
unities of time and place. The story circles round two
or three symbolic places; it does not go straggling
irregularly all over England like one of Mr. Pickwick's
coaches. People go from one place to another place;
but not from one place to another place on the road to
everywhere else. Mr. Jarndyce goes from Bleak House
to visit Mr. Boythorn; but he comes back to Bleak
House. Miss Clare and Miss Summerson go from
Bleak House to visit Mr. and Mrs. Bayham Badger;
but they come back to Bleak House. The whole
story strays from Bleak House and plunges into the
foul fogs of Chancery and the autumn mists of Chesney
Wold; but the whole story comes back to Bleak House.
The domestic title is appropriate; it is a permanent
address.

Dickens's openings are almost always good; but the
opening of *Bleak House* is good in a quite new and striking sense. Nothing could be better, for instance, than
the first foolish chapter about the genealogy of the
Chuzzlewits; but it has nothing to do with the Chuzzlewits. Nothing could be better than the first chapter
of *David Copperfield;* the breezy entrance and banging
exit of Miss Betsy Trotwood. But if there is ultimately
any crisis or serious subject-matter of *David Copperfield,*
it is the marred marriage with Dora, the final return to
Agnes; and all this is in no way involved in the highly-
amusing fact that his aunt expected him to be. a girl.
We may repeat that the matter is picaresque. The
story begins in one place and ends in another place,

and there is no real connection between the beginning
and the end except a biographical connection.

A picaresque novel is only a very eventful biography;
but the opening of *Bleak House* is quite another business altogether.   It is admirable in quite another way.
The description of the fog in the first chapter of *Bleak
House* is good in itself; but it is not merely good in itself,
like the description of the wind in the opening of *Martin
Chuzzlewit;* it is also good in the sense that Maeterlinck
is good; it is what the modern people call an atmosphere.   Dickens begins in the Chancery fog because
he means to end in the Chancery fog.   He did not begin in the Chuzzlewit wind because he meant to end in
it; he began in it because it was a good beginning.   This
is perhaps the best short way of stating the peculiarity
of the position of *Bleak House.*   In this *Bleak House*
beginning we have the feeling that it is not only a
beginning; we have the feeling that the author sees
the conclusion and the whole.   The beginning is alpha
and omega: the beginning and the end.   He means that
all the characters and all the events shall be read
through the smoky colours of that sinister and unnatural vapour.

The same is true throughout the whole tale; the
whole tale is symbolic and crowded with symbols.
Miss Flite is a funny character, like Miss La Creevy,
but Miss La Creevy means only Miss La Creevy.
Miss Flite means Chancery.   The rag-and-bone man,
Krook, is a powerful grotesque; so is Quilp; but in the
story Quilp only means Quilp; Krook means Chancery.
Rick Carstone is a kind and tragic figure, like Sidney
Carton; but Sidney Carton only means the tragedy of

human nature; Rick Carstone means the tragedy of
Chancery. Little Jo dies pathetically like Little Paul;
but for the death of Little Paul we can only blame Dickens; for the death of Little Jo we blame Chancery.
Thus the artistic unity of the book, compared to all
the author's earlier novels, is satisfying, almost suffocat-
ing. There is the *motif*, and again the *motif*. Almost
everything is calculated to assert and re-assert the
savage morality of Dickens's protest against a particular
social evil. The whole theme is that which another
Englishman as jovial as Dickens defined shortly and
finally as the law's delay. The fog of the first chapter
never lifts.

In this twilight he traced wonderful shapes. Those
people who fancy that Dickens was a mere clown; that
he could not describe anything delicate or deadly in
the human character,—those who fancy this are mostly
people whose position is explicable in many easy ways.
The vast majority of the fastidious critics have, in the
quite strict and solid sense of the words, never read
Dickens at all; hence their opposition is due to and
inspired by a hearty innocence which will certainly
make them enthusiastic Dickensians if they ever, by
some accident, happen to read him. In other cases
it is due to a certain habit of reading books under the
eye of a conventional critic, admiring what we expect
to admire, regretting what we are told to regret, waiting for Mr. Bumble to admire him, waiting for Little
Nell to despise her. Yet again, of course, it is sometimes due to that basest of all artistic indulgences
(certainly far baser than the pleasure of absinthe or
the pleasure of opium), the pleasure of appreciating

works of art which ordinary men cannot appreciate. Surely the vilest point of human vanity is exactly that; to ask to be admired for admiring what your admirers do not admire. But whatever be the reason, whether rude or subtle, which has prevented any particular man from personally admiring Dickens, there is in connection with a book like *Bleak House* something that may be called a solid and impressive challenge. Let anyone who thinks that Dickens could not describe the semi-tones and the abrupt instincts of real human nature simply take the trouble to read the stretch of chapters which detail the way in which Carstone's mind grew gradually morbid about his chances in Chancery. Let him note the manner in which the mere masculinity of Carstone is caught; how as he grows more mad he grows more logical, nay, more rational. Good women who love him come to him, and point out the fact that Jarndyce is a good man, a fact to them solid like an object of the senses. In answer he asks them to understand his position. He does not say this; he does not say that. He only urges that Jarndyce may have become cynical in the affair in the same sense that he himself may have become cynical in the affair. He is always a man; that is to say, he is always unanswerable, always wrong. The passionate certainty of the woman beats itself like battering waves against the thin smooth wall of his insane consistency. I repeat: let any one who thinks that Dickens was a gross and indelicate artist read that part of the book. If Dickens had been the clumsy journalist that such people represent, he never could have written such an episode at all. A clumsy journalist would have made

Rick Carstone in his mad career cast off Esther and
Ada and the others. The great artist knew better.
He knew that even if all the good in a man is dying,
the last sense that dies is the sense that knows a good
woman from a bad; it is like the scent of a noble
hound.

The clumsy journalist would have made Rick Carstone turn on John Jarndyce with an explosion of
hatred, as of one who had made an exposure—who had
found out what low people call "a false friend" in what
they call "his true colours." The great artist knew
better; he knew that a good man going wrong tries to
salve his soul to the last with the sense of generosity
and intellectual justice. He will try to love his enemy
if only out of mere love of himself. As the wolf dies
fighting, the good man gone wrong dies arguing.
This is what constitutes the true and real tragedy of
Richard Carstone. It is strictly the one and only
great tragedy that Dickens wrote. It is like the tragedy
of Hamlet. The others are not tragedies because they
deal almost with dead men. The tragedy of old Dorrit
is merely the sad spectacle of a dotard dragged about
Europe in his last childhood. The tragedy of Steer-
forth is only that of one who dies suddenly; the tragedy
of old Dombey only that of one who was dead all the
time. But Rick is a real tragedy, for he is still alive
when the quicksand sucks him down.

It is impossible to avoid putting in the first place
this pall of smoke which Dickens has deliberately
spread over the story. It is quite true that the country
underneath is clear enough to contain any number of
unconscious comedians or of merry monsters such as

he was in the custom of introducing into the carnival of
his tales.   But he meant us to take the smoky atmosphere seriously.   Charles Dickens, who was, like all
men who are really funny about funny things, horribly
serious about serious things, certainly meant us to
read this story in terms of his protest and his insurrec-
tion against the emptiness and arrogance of law, against
the folly and the pride of judges.   Everything else
that there is in this story entered into it through the
unconscious or accidental energy of his genius, which
broke in at every gap.   But it was the tragedy of
Richard Carstone that he meant, not the comedy of
Harold Skimpole.   He could not help being amusing;
but he meant to be depressing.

Another case might be taken as testing the greater
seriousness of this tale.   The passages about Mrs.
Jellyby and her philanthropic schemes show Dickens
at his best in his old and more familiar satiric manner.
But in the midst of the Jellyby pandemonium, which
is in itself described with the same *abandon* and irrele-
vance as the boarding-house of Mrs. Todgers or the
travelling theatre of Mr. Crummles, the elder Dickens
introduced another piece of pure truth and even tenderness.   I mean the account of Caddy Jellyby.   If
Carstone is a truly masculine study of how a man goes
wrong, Caddy is a perfectly feminine study of how a
girl goes right.   Nowhere else perhaps in fiction, and
certainly nowhere else in Dickens, is the mere female
paradox so well epitomised, the unjust use of words
covering so much capacity for a justice of ultimate
estimate; the seeming irresponsibility in language
concealing such a fixed and pitiless sense of responsibil-

ity about things; the air of being always at daggers-drawn with her own kindred, yet the confession of incurable kinship implied in pride and shame; and, above all, that thirst for order and beauty as for something physical; that strange female power of hating ugliness and waste as good men can only hate sin and bad men virtue. Every touch in her is true, from her first bewildering outbursts of hating people because she likes them, down to the sudden quietude and good sense which announces that she has slipped into her natural place as a woman. Miss Clare is a figure-head, Miss Summerson in some ways a failure; but Miss Caddy Jellyby is by far the greatest, the most human, and the most really dignified of all the heroines of Dickens.

With one or two exceptions, all the effects in this story are of this somewhat quieter kind, though none of them are so subtly successful as Rick Carstone and Caddy. Harold Skimpole begins as a sketch drawn with a pencil almost as airy and fanciful as his own. The humour of the earlier scenes is delightful—the scenes in which Skimpole looks on at other people paying his debts with the air of a kindly outsider, and suggests in formless legal phraseology that they might "sign something" or "make over something," or the scene in which he tries to explain the advantages of accepting everything to the apoplectic Mr. Boythorn. But it was one of the defects of Dickens as a novelist that his characters always became coarser and clumsier as they passed through the practical events of a story, and this would necessarily be so with Skimpole, whose position was conceivable even to himself only on the assumption that he was a mere spectator of life.

Poor Skimpole only asked to be kept out of the business of this world, and Dickens ought to have kept him out of the business of *Bleak House*. By the end of the tale he has brought Skimpole to doing acts of mere low villainy. This altogether spoils the ironical daintiness of the original notion. Skimpole was meant to end with a note of interrogation. As it is, he ends with a big, black, unmistakable blot. Speaking purely artistically, we may say that this is as great a collapse or vulgarisation as if Richard Carstone had turned into a common blackguard and wife-beater, or Caddy Jellyby into a comic and illiterate landlady. Upon the whole it may, I think, be said that the character of Skimpole is rather a piece of brilliant moralising than of pure observation or creation. Dickens had a singularly just mind. He was wild in his caricatures, but very sane in his impressions. Many of his books were devoted, and this book is partly devoted, to a denunciation of aristocracy—of the idle class that lives easily upon the toil of nations. But he was fairer than many modern revolutionists, and he insisted on satirising also those who prey on society not in the name of rank or law, but in the name of intellect and beauty. Sir Leicester Dedlock and Mr. Harold Skimpole are alike in accepting with a royal unconsciousness the anomaly and evil of their position. But the idleness and insolence of the aristocrat is human and humble compared to the idleness and insolence of the artist.

With the exception of a few fine freaks, such as Turveydrop and Chadband, all the figures in this book are touched more delicately, even more faintly, than is common with Dickens. But if the figures are touched

more faintly, it is partly because they are figures in a
fog—the fog of Chancery. Dickens meant that twilight to be oppressive; for it was the symbol of oppression. Deliberately he did not dispel the darkness
at the end of this book, as he does dispel it at the end
of most of his books. Pickwick gets out of the Fleet
Prison; Carstone never gets out of Chancery but by
death. This tyranny, Dickens said, shall not be lifted
by the light subterfuge of a fiction. This tyranny shall
never be lifted till all Englishmen lift it together.

CHILD'S HISTORY OF ENGLAND

THERE are works of great authors manifestly inferior to their typical work which are yet necessary to their fame and their figure in the world. It is not difficult to recall examples of them. No one, for instance, would talk of Scott's *Tales of a Grandfather* as indicating the power that produced *Kenilworth* and *Guy Mannering*. Nevertheless, without this chance minor compilation we should not really have the key of Scott. Without this one insignificant book we should not see his significance. For the truth was that Scott loved history more than romance, because he was so constituted as to find it more romantic than romance. He preferred the deeds of Wallace and Douglas to those of Marmion and Ivanhoe. Therefore his garrulous gossip of old times, his rambles in dead centuries, give us the real material and impulse of all his work; they represent the quarry in which he dug and the food on which he fed. Almost alone among novelists Scott actually preferred those parts of his historical novels which he had not invented himself. He exults when he can boast in an eager note that he has stolen some saying from history. Thus *The Tales of a Grandfather*, though small, is in some sense the frame of all the Waverley novels. We realise that all Scott's novels are tales of a grandfather.

What has been said here about Scott might be said

in a less degree about Thackeray's *Four Georges*. Though standing higher among his works than *The Tales of a Grandfather* among Scott's they are not his works of genius; yet they seem in some way to surround, supplement, and explain such works. Without the *Four Georges* we should know less of the link that bound Thackeray to the beginning and to the end of the eighteenth century; thence we should have known less of Colonel Esmond and also less of Lord Steyne. To these two examples I have given of the slight historical experiments of two novelists a third has to be added. The third great master of English fiction whose glory fills the nineteenth century also produced a small experiment in the popularisation of history. It is separated from the other two partly by a great difference of merit but partly also by an utter difference of tone and outlook. We seem to hear it suddenly as in the first words spoken by a new voice, a voice gay, colloquial, and impatient. Scott and Thackeray were tenderly attached to the past; Dickens (in his consciousness at any rate) was impatient with everything, but especially impatient with the past.

A collection of the works of Dickens would be incomplete in an essential as well as a literal sense without his *Child's History of England*. It may not be important as a contribution to history, but it is important as a contribution to biography; as a contribution to the character and the career of the man who wrote it, a typical man of his time. That he had made no personal historical researches, that he had no special historical learning, that he had not had, in truth, even anything that could be called a good education, all this only accentuates not the merit but at least the importance of the book. For here we may read in plain popular language, written by a man whose genius for popular exposition has never been surpassed among men, a brief account of the origin and meaning of England as it seemed to the average Englishman of that age. When subtler views of our history, some more false and some more true than his, have become popular, or at least well known, when in the near future Carlylean or Catholic or Marxian views of history have spread themselves among the reading public, this book will always remain as a bright and brisk summary of the cock-sure, healthy-minded, essentially manly and essentially ungentlemanly view of history which characterised the Radicals of that particular Radical era. The history tells us nothing about the periods that it talks about; but it tells us a great deal about the period that it does not talk about; the period in which it was written. It is in no sense a history of England from the Roman invasion; but it is certainly one of the documents which will contribute to a history of England in the nineteenth century.

Of the actual nature of its philosophical and technical limitations it is, I suppose, unnecessary to speak. They all resolve themselves into one fault common in the modern world, and certainly characteristic of historians much more learned and pretentious than Dickens. That fault consists simply in ignoring or under-rating the variety of strange evils and unique dangers in the world. The Radicals of the nineteenth century were engaged, and most righteously engaged, in dealing with one particular problem of human

civilisation; they were shifting and apportioning more
equally a load of custom that had really become unmeaning, often accidental, and nearly always unfair.
Thus, for instance, a fierce and fighting penal code,
which had been perfectly natural when the robbers
were as strong as the Government, had become in
more ordered times nothing but a base and bloody
habit. Thus again Church powers and dues, which
had been human when every man felt the Church as
the best part of himself, were mere mean privileges
when the nation was full of sects and full of free-
thinkers. This clearing away of external symbols
that no longer symbolised anything was an honourable and needful work; but it was so difficult that to
the men engaged in it it blocked up the perspective
and filled the sky, so that they slid into a very natural
mental mistake which coloured all their views of history.
They supposed that this particular problem on which
they were engaged was the one problem upon which all
mankind had always been engaged. They got it into
their heads that breaking away from a dead past was
the perpetual process of humanity. The truth is
obviously that humanity has found itself in many
difficulties very different from that. Sometimes the
best business of an age is to resist some alien invasion;
sometimes to preach practical self-control in a world
too self-indulgent and diffused; sometimes to prevent
the growth in the State of great new private enter-
prises that would poison or oppress it. Above all it
may sometimes happen that the highest task of a
thinking citizen may be to do the exact opposite of
the work which the Radicals had to do. It may be his

highest duty to cling on to every scrap of the past that he can find, if he feels that the ground is giving way beneath him and sinking into mere savagery and forgetfulness of all human culture. This was exactly the position of all thinking men in what we call the dark ages, say from the sixth to the tenth century. The cheap progressive view of history can never make head or tail of that epoch; it was an epoch upside down. We think of the old things as barbaric and the new things as enlightened. In that age all the enlightened things were old; all the barbaric and brutally ignorant things were new and up to date. Republicanism was a fading legend; despotism was a new and successful experiment. Christianity was not only better than the clans that rebelled against it; Christianity was more rationalistic than they were. When men looked back they saw progress and reason; when they looked forward they saw shapeless tradition and tribal terror. Touching such an age it is obvious that all our modern terms describing reform or conservation are foolish and beside the mark. The Conservative was then the only possible reformer. If a man did not strengthen the remains of Roman order and the root of Roman Christianity, he was simply helping the world to roll downhill into ruin and idiotcy. Remember all these evident historical truths and then turn to the account given by Charles Dickens of that great man, St. Dunstan. It is not that the pert cockney tone of the abuse is irritating to the nerves: it is that he has got the whole hang of the thing wrong. His head is full of the nineteenth-century situation; that a priest imposing discipline is a person somehow blocking the way to equality and light. Whereas the point about such a man as Dunstan was that nobody in the place except he cared a button about equality or light: and that he was defending what was left of them against the young and growing power of darkness and division and caste.

Nevertheless the case against such books as this is commonly stated wrong. The fault of Dickens is not (as is often said) that he "applies the same moral standard to all ages." Every sane man must do that: a moral standard must remain the same or it is not a moral standard. If we call St. Anthony of Padua a good man, we must mean what we mean when we call Huxley a good man, or else there is no sense in using the word "good." The fault of the Dickens school of popular history lies, not in the application of a plain rule of right and wrong to all circumstances, but in ignorance of the circumstances to which it was applied. It is not that they wrongly enforce the fixed principle that life should be saved; it is that they take a fire-engine to a shipwreck and a lifeboat to a house on fire. The business of a good man in Dickens's time was to bring justice up to date. The business of a good man in Dunstan's time was to toil to ensure the survival of any justice at all.

And Dickens, through being a living and fighting man of his own time, kept the health of his own heart, and so saw many truths with a single eye: truths that were spoilt for subtler eyes. He was much more really right than Carlyle; immeasurably more right than Froude. He was more right precisely because he applied plain human morals to all facts as he saw them.

Carlyle really had a vague idea that in coarse and cruel times it was right to be coarse and cruel; that tyranny was excusable in the twelfth century: as if the twelfth century did not denounce tyrants as much or more than any other. Carlyle, in fact, fancied that Rufus was the right sort of man; a view which was not only not shared by Anselm, but was probably not shared by Rufus. In this connection, or rather in connection with the other case of Froude, it is worth while to take another figure from Dickens's history, which illustrates the other and better side of the facile and popular method. Sheer ignorance of the environment made him wrong about Dunstan. But sheer instinct and good moral tradition made him right, for instance, about Henry VIII.; right where Froude is wildly wrong. Dickens's imagination could not re-picture an age where learning and liberty were dying rather than being born: but Henry VIII. lived in a time of expanding knowledge and unrest; a time therefore somewhat like the Victorian. And Dickens in his childish but robust way does perceive the main point about him: that he was a wicked man. He misses all the fine shades, of course; he makes him every kind of wicked man at once. He leaves out the serious interests of the man: his strange but real concern for theology; his love of certain legal and moral forms; his half-unconscious patriotism. But he sees the solid bulk of definite badness simply because it was there; and Froude cannot see it at all; because Froude followed Carlyle and played tricks with the eternal conscience. Henry VIII. *was* "a blot of blood and grease upon the history of England." For he was the embodiment of the

Devil in the Renascence, that wild worship of mere
pleasure and scorn, which with its pictures and its
palaces has enriched and ruined the world.

The time will soon come when the mere common-
sense of Dickens, like the mere common-sense of
Macaulay (though his was poisoned by learning and
Whig politics), will appear to give a plainer and therefore truer picture of the mass of history than the
mystical perversity of a man of genius writing only out
of his own temperament, like Carlyle or Taine. If a
man has a new theory of ethics there is one thing he
must not be allowed to do. Let him give laws on
Sinai, let him dictate a Bible, let him fill the world
with cathedrals if he can. But he must not be allowed
to write a history of England; or a history of any country. All history was conducted on ordinary morality:
with his extraordinary morality he is certain to read it
all askew. Thus Carlyle tries to write of the Middle
Ages with a bias against humility and mercy; that is,
with a bias against the whole theoretic morality of the
Middle Ages. The result is that he turns into a mere
turmoil of arrogant German savages what was really
the most complete and logical, if not the highest, of
human civilisations. Historically speaking, it is better
to be Dickens than to be this; better to be ignorant,
provincial, slap-dash, seeing only the passing moment,
but in that moment, to be true to eternal things.

It must be remembered, of course, that Dickens
deliberately offers this only as a "child's" history of
England. That is, he only professes to be able to
teach history as any father of a little boy of five professes to be able to teach him history. And although

the history of England would certainly be taught very differently (as regards the actual criticism of events and men) in a family with a wider culture or with another religion, the general method would be the same.   For the general method is quite right.   This black-and-white history of heroes and villains; this history full of pugnacious ethics and of nothing else, is the right kind of history for children.   I have often wondered how the scientific Marxians and the believers in "the materialist view of history" will ever manage to teach their dreary economic generalisations to children: but I suppose they will have no children.   Dickens's history will always be popular with the young; almost as popular as Dickens's novels, and for the same reason: because it is full of moralising.   Science and art without morality are not dangerous in the sense commonly supposed.   They are not dangerous like a fire, but dangerous like a fog.   A fire is dangerous in its brightness; a fog in its dulness; and thought without morals is merely dull, like a fog.   The fog seems to be creeping up the street; putting out lamp after lamp. But this cockney lamp-post which the children love is still crowned with its flame; and when the fathers have forgotten ethics, their babies will turn and teach them.

HARD TIMES

I HAVE heard that in some debating clubs there is a rule that the members may discuss anything except religion and politics. I cannot imagine what they do discuss; but it is quite evident that they have ruled out the only two subjects which are either important or amusing. The thing is a part of a certain modern tendency to avoid things because they lead to warmth; whereas, obviously, we ought, even in a social sense, to seek those things specially. The warmth of the discussion is as much a part of hospitality as the warmth of the fire. And it is singularly suggestive that in English literature the two things have died together. The very people who would blame Dickens for his sentimental hospitality are the very people who would also blame him for his narrow political conviction. The very people who would mock him for his narrow radicalism are those who would mock him for his broad fireside. Real conviction and real charity are much nearer than people suppose. Dickens was capable of loving all men; but he refused to love all opinions. The modern humanitarian can love all opinions, but he cannot love all men; he seems, sometimes, in the ecstasy of his humanitarianism, even to hate them all. He can love all opinions, including the opinion that men are unlovable.

In feeling Dickens as a lover we must never forget him as a fighter, and a fighter for a creed; but indeed there is no other kind of fighter. The geniality which he spread over all his creations was geniality spread from one centre, from one flaming peak. He was willing to excuse Mr. Micawber for being extravagant; but Dickens and Dickens's doctrine were strictly to decide how far he was to be excused. He was willing to like Mr. Twemlow in spite of his snobbishness, but Dickens and Dickens's doctrine were alone to be judges of how far he was snobbish. There was never a more didactic writer: hence there was never one more amusing. He had no mean modern notion of keeping the moral doubtful. He would have regarded this as à mere piece of slovenliness, like leaving the last page illegible.

Everywhere in Dickens's work these angles of his absolute opinion stood up out of the confusion of his general kindness, just as sharp and splintered peaks stand up out of the soft confusion of the forests. Dickens is always generous, he is generally kind-hearted, he is often sentimental, he is sometimes intolerably maudlin; but you never know when you will not come upon one of the convictions of Dickens; and when you do come upon it you do know it. It is as hard and as high as any precipice or peak of the mountains. The highest and hardest of these peaks is *Hard Times.*

It is here more than anywhere else that the sternness of Dickens emerges as separate from his softness; it is here, most obviously, so to speak, that his bones stick out. There are indeed many other books of his which are written better and written in a sadder tone. *Great Expectations* is melancholy in a sense; but it is doubtful of everything, even of its own melancholy. *The Tale of Two Cities* is a great tragedy, but it is still a sentimental tragedy. It is a great drama, but it is still a melodrama. But this tale of *Hard Times* is in some way harsher than all these. For it is the expression of a righteous indignation which cannot condescend to humour and which cannot even condescend to pathos. Twenty times we have taken Dickens's hand and it has been sometimes hot with revelry and sometimes weak with weariness; but this time we start a little, for it is inhumanly cold; and then we realise that we have touched his gauntlet of steel.

One cannot express the real value of this book without being irrelevant. It is true that one cannot express the real value of anything without being irrelevant. If we take a thing frivolously we can take it separately, but the moment we take a thing seriously, if it were only an old umbrella, it is obvious that that umbrella opens above us into the immensity of the whole universe. But there are rather particular reasons why the value of the book called *Hard Times* should be referred back to great historic and theoretic matters with which it may appear superficially to have little or nothing to do. The chief reason can perhaps be stated thus— that English politics had for more than a hundred years been getting into more and more of a hopeless tangle (a tangle which, of course, has since become even worse) and that Dickens did in some extraordinary way see what was wrong, even if he did not see what was right.

The Liberalism which Dickens and nearly all of his contemporaries professed had begun in the American and the French Revolutions. Almost all modern

English criticism upon those revolutions has been vitiated by the assumption that those revolutions burst upon a world which was unprepared for their ideas—a world ignorant of the possibility of such ideas. Somewhat the same mistake is made by those who suggest that Christianity was adopted by a world incapable of criticising it; whereas obviously it was adopted by a world that was tired of criticising everything. The vital mistake that is made about the French Revolution is merely this—that everyone talks about it as the introduction of a new idea. It was not the introduction of a new idea; there are no new ideas. Or if there are new ideas, they would not cause the least irritation if they were introduced into political society; because the world having never got used to them there would be no mass of men ready to fight for them at a moment's notice. That which was irritating about the French Revolution was this—that it was not the introduction of a new ideal, but the practical fulfilment of an old one. From the time of the first fairy tales men had always believed ideally in equality; they had always thought that something ought to be done, if anything could be done, to redress the balance between Cinderella and the ugly sisters. The irritating thing about the French was not that they said this ought to be done; everybody said that. The irritating thing about the French was that they did it. They proposed to carry out into a positive scheme what had been the vision of humanity; and humanity was naturally annoyed. The kings of Europe did not make war upon the Revolution because it was a blasphemy, but because it was a copy-book maxim which had been just too accurately copied. It was a platitude which they had always held in theory unexpectedly put into practice. The tyrants did not hate democracy because it was a paradox; they hated it because it was a truism which seemed in some danger of coming true.

Now it happens to be hugely important to have this right view of the Revolution in considering its political effects upon England. For the English, being a deeply and indeed excessively romantic people, could never be quite content with this quality of cold and bald obviousness about the republican formula. The republican formula was merely this—that the State must consist of its citizens ruling equally, however unequally they may do anything else. In their capacity of members of the State they are all equally interested in its preservation. But the English soon began to be romantically restless about this eternal truism; they were perpetually trying to turn it into something else, into something more picturesque—progress perhaps, or anarchy. At last they turned it into the highly exciting and highly unsound system of politics, which was known as the Manchester School, and which was expressed with a sort of logical flightiness, more excusable in literature, by Mr. Herbert Spencer. Of course Danton or Washington or any of the original republicans would have thought these people were mad. They would never have admitted for a moment that the State must not interfere with commerce or competition; they would merely have insisted that if the State did interfere, it must really be the State—that is, the whole people. But the distance between the common sense of Danton and the mere ecstasy of Herbert Spencer marks the English way of colouring and altering the revolutionary idea. The English people as a body went blind, as the saying is, for interpreting democracy entirely in terms of liberty. They said in substance that if they had more and more liberty it did not matter whether they had any equality or any fraternity. But this was violating the sacred trinity of true politics; they confounded the persons and they divided the substance.

Now the really odd thing about England in the nineteenth century is this—that there was one Englishman who happened to keep his head. The men who lost their heads lost highly scientific and philosophical heads; they were great cosmic systematisers like Spencer, great social philosophers like Bentham, great practical politicians like Bright, great political economists like Mill. The man who kept his head kept a head full of fantastic nonsense; he was a writer of rowdy farces, a demagogue of fiction, a man without education in any serious sense whatever, a man whose whole business was to turn ordinary cockneys into extraordinary caricatures. Yet when all these other children of the revolution went wrong he, by a mystical something in his bones, went right. He knew nothing of the Revolution; yet he struck the note of it. He returned to the original sentimental commonplace upon which it is forever founded, as the Church is founded on a rock. In an England gone mad about a minor theory he reasserted the original idea—the idea that no one in the State must be too weak to influence the State.

This man was Dickens. He did this work much more genuinely than it was done by Carlyle or Ruskin;

for they were simply Tories making out a romantic case
for the return of Toryism. But Dickens was a real
Liberal demanding the return of real Liberalism.
Dickens was there to remind people that England had
rubbed out two words of the revolutionary motto, had
left only Liberty and destroyed Equality and Fraternity.
In this book, *Hard Times*, he specially champions
equality. In all his books he champions fraternity.

The atmosphere of this book and what it stands for
can be very adequately conveyed in the note on the
book by Lord Macaulay, who may stand as a very good
example of the spirit of England in those years of eager
emancipation and expanding wealth—the years in
which Liberalism was turned from an omnipotent truth
to a weak scientific system. Macaulay's private comment on *Hard Times* runs, "One or two passages of
exquisite pathos and the rest sullen Socialism." That
is not an unfair and certainly not a specially hostile
criticism, but it exactly shows how the book struck
those people who were mad on political liberty and
dead about everything else. Macaulay mistook for a
new formula called Socialism what was, in truth, only
the old formula called political democracy. He and his
Whigs had so thoroughly mauled and modified the
original idea of Rousseau or Jefferson that when they
saw it again they positively thought that it was something quite new and eccentric. But the truth was that
Dickens was not a Socialist, but an unspoilt Liberal; he
was not sullen; nay, rather, he had remained strangely
hopeful. They called him a sullen Socialist only to
disguise their astonishment at finding still loose about
the London streets a happy republican.

Dickens is the one living link between the old kindness and the new, between the good will of the past and the good works of the future. He links May Day with Bank Holiday, and he does it almost alone. All the men around him, great and good as they were, were in comparison puritanical, and never so puritanical as when they were also atheistic. He is a sort of solitary pipe down which pours to the twentieth century the original river of Merry England. And although this *Hard Times* is, as its name implies, the hardest of his works, although there is less in it perhaps than in any of the others of the *abandon* and the buffoonery of Dickens, this only emphasises the more clearly the fact that he stood almost alone for a more humane and hilarious view of democracy. None of his great and much more highly-educated contemporaries could help him in this. Carlyle was as gloomy on the one side as Herbert Spencer on the other. He protested against the commercial oppression simply and solely because it was not only an oppression but a depression. And this protest of his was made specially in the case of the book before us. It may be bitter, but it was a protest against bitterness. It may be dark, but it is the darkness of the subject and not of the author. He is by his own account dealing with hard times, but not with a hard eternity, not with a hard philosophy of the universe. Nevertheless, this is the one place in his work where he does not make us remember human happiness by example as well as by precept. This is, as I have said, not the saddest, but certainly the harshest of his stories. It is perhaps the only place where Dickens, in defending happiness, for a moment forgets to be happy.

He describes Bounderby and Gradgrind with a degree
of grimness and sombre hatred very different from the
half affectionate derision which he directed against the
old tyrants or humbugs of the earlier nineteenth century
—the pompous Dedlock or the fatuous Nupkins, the
grotesque Bumble or the inane Tigg. In those old
books his very abuse was benignant; in *Hard Times*
even his sympathy is hard. And the reason is again to
be found in the political facts of the century. Dickens
could be half genial with the older generation of oppressors because it was a dying generation. It was
evident, or at least it seemed evident then, that Nupkins
could not go on much longer making up the law of
England to suit himself; that Sir Leicester Dedlock
could not go on much longer being kind to his tenants
as if they were dogs and cats. And some of these evils
the nineteenth century did really eliminate or improve.
For the first half of the century Dickens and all his
friends were justified in feeling that the chains were
falling from mankind. At any rate, the chains did
fall from Mr. Rouncewell the Iron-master. And
when they fell from him he picked them up and put
them upon the poor.

LITTLE DORRIT

Little Dorrit stands in Dickens's life chiefly as a signal of how far he went down the road of realism, of sadness, and of what is called modernity. True, it was by no means the best of the books of his later period; some even think it the worst. *Great Expectations* is certainly the best of the later novels; some even think it the best of all the novels. Nor is it the novel most concerned with strictly recent problems; that title must be given to *Hard Times*. Nor again is it the most finely finished or well constructed of the later books; that claim can be probably made for *Edwin Drood*. By a queer verbal paradox the most carefully finished of his later tales is the tale that is not finished at all. In form, indeed, the book bears a superficial resemblance to those earlier works by which the young Dickens had set the whole world laughing long ago. Much of the story refers to a remote time early in the nineteenth century; much of it was actually recalled and copied from the life of Dickens's father in the old Marshalsea prison. Also the narrative has something of the form, or rather absence of form, which belonged to *Nicholas Nickleby* or *Martin Chuzzlewit*. It has something of the old air of being a string of disconnected adventures, like a boy's book about bears and Indians. The Dorrits go wandering for no particular reason on the Continent of Europe, just as young Martin Chuzzlewit went wandering for no particular reason on the continent of America. The story of *Little Dorrit* stops and lingers at the doors of the Circumlocution Office much in the same way that the story of Samuel Pickwick stops and lingers in the political excitement of Eatanswill. The villain, Blandois, is a very stagey villain indeed; quite as stagey as Ralph Nickleby or the mysterious Monk. The secret of the dark house of Clennam is a very silly secret; quite as silly as the secret of Ralph Nickleby or the secret of Monk. Yet all these external similarities between *Little Dorrit* and the earliest books, all this loose, melodramatic quality, only serves to make more obvious and startling the fact that some change has come over the soul of Dickens. *Hard Times* is harsh; but then *Hard Times* is a social pamphlet; perhaps it is only harsh as a social pamphlet must be harsh. *Bleak House* is a little sombre; but then *Bleak House* is almost a detective story; perhaps it is only sombre in the sense that a detective story must be sombre. *A Tale of Two Cities* is a tragedy; but then *A Tale of Two Cities* is a tale of the French Revolution; perhaps it is only a tragedy because the French Revolution was a tragedy. *The Mystery of Edwin Drood* is dark; but then the mystery of anybody must be dark. In all these other cases of the later books an artistic reason can be given—a reason of theme or of construction for the slight sadness that seems to cling to them. But exactly because *Little Dorrit* is a mere Dickens novel, it shows that something must somehow have happened to Dickens himself. Even in resuming his old liberty, he cannot resume his old hilarity. He can re-create the anarchy, but not the revelry.

It so happens that this strange difference between the new and the old mode of Dickens can be symbolised and stated in one separate and simple contrast. Dickens's father had been a prisoner in a debtors' prison, and Dickens's works contain two pictures partly suggested by the personality of that prisoner. Mr. Micawber is one picture of him. Mr. Dorrit is another. This truth is almost incredible, but it is the truth. The joyful Micawber, whose very despair was exultant, and the desolate Dorrit, whose very pride was pitiful, were the same man. The valiant Micawber and the nervous, shaking Dorrit were the same man. The defiant Micawber and the snobbish, essentially obsequious Dorrit were the same man. I do not mean of course that either of the pictures was an exact copy of anybody. The whole Dickens genius consisted of taking hints and turning them into human beings. As he took twenty real persons and turned them into one fictitious person, so he took one real person and turned him into twenty fictitious persons. This quality would suggest one character, that quality would suggest another. But in this case, at any rate, he did take one real person and turn him into two. And what is more, he turned him into two persons who seem to be quite opposite persons. To ordinary readers of Dickens, to say that Micawber and Dorrit had in any sense the same original, will appear unexpected and wild. No conceivable connection between the two would ever have occurred to anybody who had read Dickens with simple and superficial enjoyment, as all good literature ought to be read.

It will seem to them just as silly as saying that the Fat
Boy and Mr. Alfred Jingle were both copied from the
same character. It will seem as insane as saying that
the character of Smike and the character of Major
Bagstock were both copied from Dickens's father.
Yet it is an unquestionable historical fact that Micawber
and Dorrit were both copied from Dickens's father,
in the only sense that any figures in good literature are
ever copied from anything or anybody. Dickens did
get the main idea of Micawber from his father; and
that idea is that a poor man is not conquered by the
world. And Dickens did get the main idea of Dorrit
from his father; and that idea is that a poor man may
be conquered by the world. I shall take the opportunity of discussing, in a moment, which of these ideas
is true. Doubtless old John Dickens included both the
gay and the sad moral; most men do. My only purpose
here is to point out that Dickens drew the gay moral
in 1849, and the sad moral in 1857.

There must have been some real sadness at this time
creeping like a cloud over Dickens himself. It is nothing that a man dwells on the darkness of dark things;
all healthy men do that. It is when he dwells on the
darkness of bright things that we have reason to fear
some disease of the emotions. There must really have
been some depression when a man can only see the sad
side of flowers or the sad side of holidays or the sad side
of wine. And there must be some depression of an
uncommonly dark and genuine character when a man
has reached such a point that he can see only the sad
side of Mr. Wilkins Micawber.

Yet this is in reality what had happened to Dickens

about this time. Staring at Wilkins Micawber he
could see only the weakness and the tragedy that was
made possible by his indifference, his indulgence, and
his bravado. He had already indeed been slightly
moved towards this study of the feebleness and ruin of
the old epicurean type with which he had once sympathised, the type of Bob Sawyer or Dick Swiveller.
He had already attacked the evil of it in *Bleak House*
in the character of Harold Skimpole, with its essentially
cowardly carelessness and its highly selfish communism.
Nevertheless, as I have said before, it must have been
no small degree of actual melancholia which led Dickens
to look for a lesson of disaster and slavery in the very
same career from which he had once taught lessons of
continual recuperation and a kind of fantastic freedom.
There must have been at this time some melancholy
behind the writings. There must have existed on this
earth at the time that portent and paradox—a somewhat depressed Dickens.

Perhaps it was a reminiscence of that metaphorical
proverb which tells us that "truth lies at the bottom
of a well." Perhaps these people thought that the only
way to find truth in the well was to drown oneself.
But on whatever thin theoretic basis, the type and period
of George Gissing did certainly consider that Dickens,
so far as he went, was all the worse for the optimism
of the story of Micawber; hence it is not unnatural that
they should think him all the better for the comparative
pessimism of the story of *Little Dorrit*. The very things
in the tale that would naturally displease the ordinary
admirers of Dickens, are the things which would naturally please a man like George Gissing. There are

many of these things, but one of them emerges pre-eminent and unmistakable. This is the fact that when all is said and done the main business of the story of *Little Dorrit* is to describe the victory of circumstances over a soul. The circumstances are the financial ruin and long imprisonment of Edward Dorrit; the soul is Edward Dorrit himself. Let it be granted that the circumstances are exceptional and oppressive, are denounced as exceptional and oppressive, are finally exploded and overthrown; still, they are circumstances. Let it be granted that the soul is that of a man perhaps weak in any case and retaining many merits to the last, still it is a soul. Let it be granted, above all, that the admission that such spiritual tragedies do occur does not decrease by so much as an iota our faith in the validity of any spiritual struggle. For example, Stevenson has made a study of the breakdown of a good man's character under a burden for which he is not to blame, in the tragedy of Henry Durie in *The Master of Ballantrae*. Yet he has added, in the mouth of Mackellar, the exact common sense and good theology of the matter, saying "It matters not a jot; for he that is to pass judgment upon the records of our life is the same that formed us in frailty." Let us concede then all this, and the fact remains that the study of the slow demoralisation of a man through mere misfortune was not a study congenial to Dickens, not in accordance with his original inspiration, not connected in any manner with the special thing that he had to say. In a word, the thing is not quite a part of himself; and he was not quite himself when he did it.

He was still quite a young man; his depression did not

come from age. In fact, as far as I know, mere depression never does come from mere age. Age can pass into a beautiful reverie. Age can pass into a sort of beautiful idiocy. But I do not think that the actual decline and close of our ordinary vitality brings with it any particular heaviness of the spirits. The spirits of the old do not as a rule seem to become more and more ponderous until they sink into the earth. Rather the spirits of the old seem to grow lighter and lighter until they float away like thistledown. Wherever there is the definite phenomenon called depression, it commonly means that something else has been closer to us than so normal a thing as death. There has been disease, bodily or mental, or there has been sin, or there has been some struggle or effort, breaking past the ordinary boundaries of human custom. In the case of Dickens there had been two things that are not of the routine of a wholesome human life; there had been the quarrel with his wife, and there had been the strain of incessant and exaggerated intellectual labour. He had not an easy time; and on top of that (or perhaps rather at the bottom of it) he had not an easy nature. Not only did his life necessitate work, but his character necessitated worry about work; and that combination is always one which is very dangerous to the temperament which is exposed to it. The only people who ought to be allowed to work are the people who are able to shirk. The only people who ought to be allowed to worry are the people who have nothing to worry about. When the two are combined, as they were in Dickens, you are very likely to have at least one collapse. *Little Dorrit* is a very interesting, sincere, and fascinating book. But for all that, I fancy it is the one collapse.

The complete proof of this depression may be difficult to advance; because it will be urged, and entirely with reason, that the actual examples of it are artistic and appropriate. Dickens, the Gissing school will say, was here pointing out certain sad truths of psychology; can any one say that he ought not to point them out? That may be; in any case, to explain depression is not to remove it. But the instances of this more sombre quality of which I have spoken are not very hard to find. The thing can easily be seen by comparing a book like *Little Dorrit* with a book like *David Copperfield*. David Copperfield and Arthur Clennam have both been brought up in unhappy homes, under bitter guardians and a black, disheartening religion. It is the whole point of David Copperfield that he has broken out of a Calvinistic tyranny which he cannot forgive. But it is the whole point of Arthur Clennam that he has not broken out of the Calvinistic tyranny, but is still under its shadow. Copperfield has come from a gloomy childhood; Clennam, though forty years old, is still in a gloomy childhood. When David meets the Murdstones again it is to defy them with the health and hilarious anger that go with his happy delirium about Dora. But when Clennam re-enters his sepulchral house there is a weight upon his soul which makes it impossible for him to answer, with any spirit, the morbidities of his mother, or even the grotesque interferences of Mr. Flintwinch. This is only another example of the same quality which makes the Dickens of *Little Dorrit* insist on the degradation of the debtor, while the Dickens of *David Copperfield* insisted on his splendid irresponsibility, his essential emancipation. Imprisonments passed over Micawber like summer clouds.   But the imprisonment in *Little Dorrit* is like a complete natural climate and environment; it has positively modified the shapes and functions of the animals that dwell in it.   A horrible thing has happened to Dickens; he has almost become an Evolutionist. Worse still, in studying the Calvinism of Mrs. Clennam's house, he has almost become a Calvinist.   He half believes (as do some of the modern scientists) that there is really such a thing as "a child of wrath," that a man on whom such an early shadow had fallen could never shake it off.   For ancient Calvinism and modern Evolutionism are essentially the same things.   They are both ingenious logical blasphemies against the dignity and liberty of the human soul.

The workmanship of the book in detail is often extremely good.   The one passage in the older and heartier Dickens manner (I mean the description of the Circumlocution Office) is beyond praise.   It is a complete picture of the way England is actually governed at this moment.   The very core of our politics is expressed in the light and easy young Barnacle who told Clennam with a kindly frankness that he, Clennam, would "never go on with it."   Dickens hit the mark so that the bell rang when he made all the lower officials, who were cads, tell Clennam coldly that his claim was absurd, until the last official, who is a gentleman, tells him genially that the whole business is absurd.   Even here, perhaps, there is something more than the old exuberant derision of Dickens; there is a touch of experience that verges on scepticism.

Everywhere else, certainly, there is the note which I have called Calvinistic; especially in the predestined passion of Tattycoram or the incurable cruelty of Miss Wade. Even Little Dorrit herself had, we are told, one stain from her prison experience; and it is spoken of like a bodily stain; like something that cannot be washed away.

There is no denying that this is Dickens's dark moment. It adds enormously to the value of his general view of life that such a dark moment came. He did what all the heroes and all the really happy men have done; he descended into Hell. Nor is it irreverent to continue the quotation from the Creed, for in the next book he was to write he was to break out of all these dreams of fate and failure, and with his highest voice to speak of the triumph of the weak of this world. His next book was to leave us saying, as Sydney Carton mounted the scaffold, words which, splendid in themselves, have never been so splendidly quoted—"I am the Resurrection and the Life; whoso believeth in Me though he be dead yet he shall live." In Sydney Carton at least, Dickens shows none of that dreary submission to the environment of the irrevocable that had for an instant lain on him like a cloud. On this occasion he sees with the old heroic clearness that to be a failure may be one step to being a saint. On the third day he rose again from the dead.

A TALE OF TWO CITIES

As an example of Dickens's literary work, *A Tale of Two Cities* is not wrongly named. It is his most typical contact with the civic ideals of Europe. All his other tales have been tales of one city. He was in spirit a Cockney; though that title has been quite unreasonably twisted to mean a cad. By the old sound and proverbial test a Cockney was a man born within the sound of Bow bells. That is, he was a man born within the immediate appeal of high civilisation and of eternal religion. Shakespeare, in the heart of his fantastic forest, turns with a splendid suddenness to the Cockney ideal as being the true one after all. For a jest, for a reaction, for an idle summer love or still idler summer hatred, it is well to wander away into the bewildering forest of Arden. It is well that those who are sick with love or sick with the absence of love, those who weary of the folly of courts or weary yet more of their wisdom, it is natural that these should trail away into the twinkling twilight of the woods. Yet it is here that Shakespeare makes one of his most arresting and startling assertions of the truth. Here is one of those rare and tremendous moments of which one may say that there is a stage direction, "Enter Shakespeare." He has admitted that for men weary of courts, for men sick of cities, the wood is the wisest place, and he has

praised it with his purest lyric ecstasy. But when a
man enters suddenly upon that celestial picnic, a man
who is not sick of cities, but sick of hunger, a man who
is not weary of courts, but weary of walking, then
Shakespeare lets through his own voice with a shatter-
ing sincerity and cries the praise of practical human
civilisation:

> If ever you have looked on better days,
> If ever you have sat at good men's feasts,
> If ever been where bells have knolled to church,
> If ever from your eyelids wiped a tear
> Or know what 't is to pity and be pitied.

There is nothing finer even in Shakespeare than that
conception of the circle of rich men all pretending to
rough it in the country, and the one really hungry man
entering, sword in hand, and praising the city. "If
ever been where bells have knolled to church"; if you
have ever been within sound of Bow bells; if you have
ever been happy and haughty enough to call yourself a
Cockney.

We must remember this distinction always in the
case of Dickens. Dickens is the great Cockney, at
once tragic and comic, who enters abruptly upon the
Arcadian banquet of the æsthetics and says, "Forbear
and eat no more," and tells them that they shall not
eat "until necessity be served." If there was one
thing he would have favoured instinctively it would
have been the spreading of the town as meaning the
spreading of civilisation. And we should (I hope) all
favour the spreading of the town if it did mean the
spreading of civilisation. The objection to the spread-

ing of the modern Manchester or Birmingham suburb is simply that such a suburb is much more barbaric than any village in Europe could ever conceivably be. And again, if there is anything that Dickens would have definitely hated it is that general treatment of nature as a dramatic spectacle, a piece of scene-painting which has become the common mark of the culture of our wealthier classes. Despite many fine pictures of natural scenery, especially along the English road-sides, he was upon the whole emphatically on the side of the town. He was on the side of bricks and mortar. He was a citizen; and, after all, a citizen means a man of the city. His strength was, after all, in the fact that he was a man of the city. But, after all, his weakness, his calamitous weakness, was that he was a man of one city.

For all practical purposes he had never been outside such places as Chatham and London. He did indeed travel on the Continent; but surely no man's travel was ever so superficial as his. He was more superficial than the smallest and commonest tourist. He went about Europe on stilts; he never touched the ground. There is one good test and one only of whether a man has travelled to any profit in Europe. An Englishman is, as such, a European, and as he approaches the central splendours of Europe he ought to feel that he is coming home. If he does not feel at home he had much better have stopped at home. England is a real home; London is a real home; and all the essential feelings of adventure or the picturesque can easily be gained by going out at night upon the flats of Essex or the cloven hills of Surrey. Your visit to Europe is useless unless

it gives you the sense of an exile returning. Your first
sight of Rome is futile unless you feel that you have
seen it before. Thus useless and thus futile were the
foreign experiments and the continental raids of
Dickens. He enjoyed them as he would have enjoyed,
as a boy, a scamper out of Chatham into some strange
meadows, as he would have enjoyed, when a grown
man, a steam in a police boat out into the fens to the far
east of London. But he was the Cockney venturing
far; he was not the European coming home. He is
still the splendid Cockney Orlando of whom I spoke
above; he cannot but suppose that any strange men,
being happy in some pastoral way, are mysterious
foreign scoundrels. Dickens's real speech to the lazy
and laughing civilisation of Southern Europe would
really have run in the Shakespearian words:

> but whoe'er you be
Who in this desert inaccessible,
Under the shade of melancholy boughs
Lose and neglect the creeping hours of time.
If ever you have looked on better things,
If ever been where bells have knolled to church.

If, in short, you have ever had the advantage of being
born within the sound of Bow bells. Dickens could not
really conceive that there was any other city but his
own.

It is necessary thus to insist that Dickens never
understood the Continent, because only thus can we
appreciate the really remarkable thing he did in *A
Tale of Two Cities*. It is necessary to feel, first of all,
the fact that to him London was the centre of the uni-

verse. He did not understand at all the real sense in which Paris is the capital of Europe. He had never realised that all roads lead to Rome. He had never felt (as an Englishman can feel) that he was an Athenian before he was a Londoner. Yet with everything against him he did this astonishing thing. He wrote a book about two cities, one of which he understood; the other he did not understand. And his description of the city he did not know is almost better than his description of the city he did know. This is the entrance of the unquestionable thing about Dickens; the thing called genius; the thing which every one has to talk about directly and distinctly because no one knows what it is. For a plain word (as for instance the word fool) always covers an infinite mystery.

A Tale of Two Cities is one of the more tragic tints of the later life of Dickens. It might be said that he grew sadder as he grew older; but this would be false, for two reasons. First, a man never or hardly ever does grow sad as he grows old; on the contrary, the most melancholy young lovers can be found forty years afterwards chuckling over their port wine. And second, Dickens never did grow old, even in a physical sense. What weariness did appear in him appeared in the prime of life; it was due not to age but to overwork, and his exaggerative way of doing everything. To call Dickens a victim of elderly disenchantment would be as absurd as to say the same of Keats. Such fatigue as there was, was due not to the slowing down of his blood, but rather to its unremitting rapidity. He was not wearied by his age; rather he was wearied by his youth. And though *A Tale of Two Cities* is full

of sadness, it is full also of enthusiasm; that pathos
is a young pathos rather than an old one. Yet there
is one circumstance which does render important the
fact that *A Tale of Two Cities* is one of the later works
of Dickens. This fact is the fact of his dependence
upon another of the great writers of the Victorian era.
And it is in connection with this that we can best see
the truth of which I have been speaking; the truth that
his actual ignorance of France went with amazing
intuitive perception of the truth about it. It is here
that he has most clearly the plain mark of the man
of genius; that he can understand what he does not
understand.

Dickens was inspired to the study of the French
Revolution and to the writing of a romance about it
by the example and influence of Carlyle. Thomas
Carlyle undoubtedly rediscovered for Englishmen the
revolution that was at the back of all their policies
and reforms. It is an entertaining side joke that the
French Revolution should have been discovered for
Britons by the only British writer who did not really
believe in it. Nevertheless, the most authoritative
and the most recent critics on that great renaissance
agree in considering Carlyle's work one of the most
searching and detailed power. Carlyle had read a great
deal about the French Revolution. Dickens had read
nothing at all, except Carlyle. Carlyle was a man who
collected his ideas by the careful collation of documents
and the verification of references. Dickens was a
man who collected his ideas from loose hints in the
streets, and those always the same streets; as I have
said, he was the citizen of one city. Carlyle was in his

way learned; Dickens was in every way ignorant.
Dickens was an Englishman cut off from France;
Carlyle was a Scotsman, historically connected with
France. And yet, when all this is said and certified,
Dickens is more right than Carlyle. Dickens's French
Revolution is probably more like the real French
Revolution than Carlyle's. It is difficult, if not impossible, to state the grounds of this strong conviction.
One can only talk of it by employing that excellent
method which Cardinal Newman employed when
he spoke of the "notes" of Catholicism. There were
certain "notes" of the Revolution. One note of the
Revolution was the thing which silly people call optimism, and sensible people call high spirits. Carlyle
could never quite get it, because with all his spiritual
energy he had no high spirits. That is why he preferred
prose to poetry. He could understand rhetoric; for
rhetoric means singing with an object. But he could
not understand lyrics; for the lyric means singing without an object; as every one does when he is happy.
Now for all its blood and its black guillotines, the French
Revolution was full of mere high spirits. Nay, it was
full of happiness. This actual lilt and levity Carlyle
never really found in the Revolution, because he could
not find it in himself. Dickens knew less of the Revolution, but he had more of it. When Dickens attacked
abuses, he battered them down with exactly that sort of
cheery and quite one-sided satisfaction with which the
French mob battered down the Bastille. Dickens
utterly and innocently believed in certain things;
he would, I think, have drawn the sword for them.
Carlyle half believed in half a hundred things; he was at

once more of a mystic and more of a sceptic. Carlyle
was the perfect type of the grumbling servant; the old
grumbling servant of the aristocratic comedies. He
followed the aristocracy, but he growled as he followed.
He was obedient without being servile, just as Caleb
Balderstone was obedient without being servile. But
Dickens was the type of the man who might really
have rebelled instead of grumbling. He might have
gone out into the street and fought, like the man who
took the Bastille. It is somewhat nationally significant
that when we talk of the man in the street it means a
figure silent, slouching, and even feeble. When the
French speak of the man in the street, it means danger
in the street.

No one can fail to notice this deep difference between
Dickens and the Carlyle whom he avowedly copied.
Splendid and symbolic as are Carlyle's scenes of the
French Revolution, we have in reading them a curious
sense that everything is happening at night. In
Dickens even massacre happens by daylight. Carlyle
always assumes that because things were tragedies
therefore the men who did them felt tragic. Dickens
knows that the man who works the worst tragedies is
the man who feels comic; as for example, Mr. Quilp.
The French Revolution was a much simpler world than
Carlyle could understand; for Carlyle was subtle and
not simple. Dickens could understand it, for he was
simple and not subtle. He understood that plain rage
against plain political injustice; he understood again
that obvious vindictiveness and that obvious brutality
which followed. "Cruelty and the abuse of absolute
power," he told an American slave-owner, "are two of

the bad passions of human nature." Carlyle was quite incapable of rising to the height of that uplifted common-sense. He must always find something mystical about the cruelty of the French Revolution. The effect was equally bad whether he found it mystically bad and called the thing anarchy, or whether he found it mystically good and called it the rule of the strong. In both cases he could not understand the common-sense justice or the common-sense vengeance of Dickens and the French Revolution.

Yet Dickens has in this book given a perfect and final touch to this whole conception of mere rebellion and mere human nature. Carlyle had written the story of the French Revolution and had made the story a mere tragedy. Dickens writes the story about the French Revolution, and does not make the Revolution itself the tragedy at all. Dickens knows that an outbreak is seldom a tragedy; generally it is the avoidance of a tragedy. All the real tragedies are silent. Men fight each other with furious cries, because men fight each other with chivalry and an unchangeable sense of brotherhood. But trees fight each other in utter stillness; because they fight each other cruelly and without quarter. In this book, as in history, the guillotine is not the calamity, but rather the solution of the calamity. The sin of Sydney Carton is a sin of habit, not of revolution. His gloom is the gloom of London, not the gloom of Paris.

GREAT EXPECTATIONS

Great Expectations, which was written in the afternoon of Dickens's life and fame, has a quality of serene irony and even sadness, which puts it quite alone among his other works. At no time could Dickens possibly be called cynical, he had too much vitality; but relatively to the other books this book is cynical; but it has the soft and gentle cynicism of old age, not the hard cynicism of youth. To be a young cynic is to be a young brute; but Dickens, who had been so perfectly romantic and sentimental in his youth, could afford to admit this touch of doubt into the mixed experience of his middle age. At no time could any books by Dickens have been called Thackerayan. Both of the two men were too great for that. But relatively to the other Dickensian productions this book may be called Thackerayan. It is a study in human weakness and the slow human surrender. It describes how easily a free lad of fresh and decent instincts can be made to care more for rank and pride and the degrees of our stratified society than for old affection and for honour. It is an extra chapter to *The Book of Snobs*.

The best way of stating the change which this book marks in Dickens can be put in one phrase. In this book for the first time the hero disappears. The hero had descended to Dickens by a long line which begins with the gods, nay, perhaps if one may say so, which begins with God. First comes Deity and then the image of Deity; first comes the god and then the demi-god, the Hercules who labours and conquers before he receives his heavenly crown. That idea, with continual mystery and modification, has continued behind all romantic tales; the demi-god became the hero of paganism; the hero of paganism became the knight-errant of Christianity; the knight-errant who wandered and was foiled before he triumphed became the hero of the later prose romance, the romance in which the hero had to fight a duel with the villain but always survived, in which the hero drove desperate horses through the night in order to rescue the heroine, but always rescued her.

This heroic modern hero, this demi-god in a top-hat, may be said to reach his supreme moment and typical example about the time when Dickens was writing that thundering and thrilling and highly unlikely scene in *Nicholas Nickleby*, the scene where Nicholas hopelessly denounces the atrocious Gride in his hour of grinning triumph, and a thud upon the floor above tells them that the heroine's tyrannical father has died just in time to set her free. That is the apotheosis of the pure heroic as Dickens found it, and as Dickens in some sense continued it. It may be that it does not appear with quite so much unmistakable youth, beauty, valour, and virtue as it does in Nicholas Nickleby. Walter Gay is a simpler and more careless hero, but when he is doing any of the business of the story he is purely heroic. Kit Nubbles is a humbler hero, but he is a hero; when he is good he is very good. Even

David Copperfield, who confesses to boyish tremors and boyish evasions in his account of his boyhood, acts the strict stiff part of the chivalrous gentleman in all the active and determining scenes of the tale. But *Great Expectations* may be called, like *Vanity Fair*, a novel without a hero. Almost all Thackeray's novels except *Esmond* are novels without a hero, but only one of Dickens's novels can be so described. I do not mean that it is a novel without a *jeune premier*, a young man to make love; *Pickwick* is that and *Oliver Twist*, and, perhaps, *The Old Curiosity Shop*. I mean that it is a novel without a hero in the same far deeper and more deadly sense in which *Pendennis* is also a novel without a hero. I mean that it is a novel which aims chiefly at showing that the hero is unheroic.

All such phrases as these must appear of course to overstate the case. Pip is a much more delightful person than Nicholas Nickleby. Or to take a stronger case for the purpose of our argument, Pip is a much more delightful person than Sydney Carton. Still the fact remains. Most of Nicholas Nickleby's personal actions are meant to show that he is heroic. Most of Pip's actions are meant to show that he is not heroic. The study of Sydney Carton is meant to indicate that with all his vices Sydney Carton was a hero. The study of Pip is meant to indicate that with all his virtues Pip was a snob. The motive of the literary explanation is different. Pip and Pendennis are meant to show how circumstances can corrupt men. Sam Weller and Hercules are meant to show how heroes can subdue circumstances.

This is the preliminary view of the book which is

necessary if we are to regard it as a real and separate fact in the life of Dickens. Dickens had many moods because he was an artist; but he had one great mood, because he was a great artist. Any real difference therefore from the general drift, or rather (I apologise to Dickens) the general drive of his creation is very important. This is the one place in his work in which he does, I will not say feel like Thackeray, far less think like Thackeray, less still write like Thackeray, but this is the one of his works in which he understands Thackeray. He puts himself in some sense in the same place; he considers mankind at somewhat the same angle as mankind is considered in one of the sociable and sarcastic novels of Thackeray. When he deals with Pip he sets out not to show his strength like the strength of Hercules, but to show his weakness like the weakness of Pendennis. When he sets out to describe Pip's great expectation he does not set out, as in a fairy tale, with the idea that these great expectations will be fulfilled; he sets out from the first with the idea that these great expectations will be disappointing. We might very well, as I have remarked elsewhere, apply to all Dickens's books the title *Great Expectations*. All his books are full of an airy and yet ardent expectation of everything; of the next person who shall happen to speak, of the next chimney that shall happen to smoke, of the next event, of the next ecstasy; of the next fulfilment of any eager human fancy. All his books might be called *Great Expectations*. But the only book to which he gave the name of *Great Expectations* was the only book in which the expectation was never realised. It was so with the whole of that splendid and unconscious generation to which he belonged. The whole glory of that old English middle class was that it was unconscious; its excellence was entirely in that, that it was the culture of the nation, and that it did not know it. If Dickens had ever known that he was optimistic, he would have ceased to be happy.

It is necessary to make this first point clear: that in *Great Expectations* Dickens was really trying to be a quiet, a detached, and even a cynical observer of human life. Dickens was trying to be Thackeray. And the final and startling triumph of Dickens is this: that even to this moderate and modern story, he gives an incomparable energy which is not moderate and which is not modern. He is trying to be reasonable; but in spite of himself he is inspired. He is trying to be detailed, but in spite of himself he is gigantic. Compared to the rest of Dickens this is Thackeray; but compared to the whole of Thackeray we can only say in supreme praise of it that it is Dickens.

Take, for example, the one question of snobbishness. Dickens has achieved admirably the description of the doubts and vanities of the wretched Pip as he walks down the street in his new gentlemanly clothes, the clothes of which he is so proud and so ashamed. Nothing could be so exquisitely human, nothing especially could be so exquisitely masculine as that combination of self-love and self-assertion and even insolence with a naked and helpless sensibility to the slightest breath of ridicule. Pip thinks himself better than every one else, and yet anybody can snub him; that is the everlasting male, and perhaps the everlasting gentleman. Dickens has described perfectly this quivering and defenceless dignity. Dickens has described perfectly how ill-armed it is against the coarse humour of real humanity—the real humanity which Dickens loved, but which idealists and philanthropists do not love, the humanity of cabmen and costermongers and men singing in a third-class carriage; the humanity of Trabb's boy. In describing Pip's weakness Dickens is as true and as delicate as Thackeray. But Thackeray might have been easily as true and as delicate as Dickens. This quick and quiet eye for the tremors of mankind is a thing which Dickens possessed, but which others possessed also. George Eliot or Thackeray could have described the weakness of Pip. Exactly what George Eliot and Thackeray could not have described was the vigour of Trabb's boy. There would have been admirable humour and observation in their accounts of that intolerable urchin. Thackeray would have given us little light touches of Trabb's boy, absolutely true to the quality and colour of the humour, just as in his novels of the eighteenth century, the glimpses of Steele or Bolingbroke or Doctor Johnson are exactly and perfectly true to the colour and quality of their humour. George Eliot in her earlier books would have given us shrewd authentic scraps of the real dialect of Trabb's boy, just as she gave us shrewd and authentic scraps of the real talk in a Midland country town. In her later books she would have given us highly rationalistic explanations of Trabb's boy; which we should not have read. But exactly what they could never have given, and exactly what Dickens does give, is the *bounce* of Trabb's boy. It is the real unconquerable rush and energy in a character which was the supreme and quite

indescribable greatness of Dickens. He conquered
by rushes; he attacked in masses; he carried things
at the spear point in a charge of spears; he was the
Rupert of Fiction. The thing about any figure of
Dickens, about Sam Weller or Dick Swiveller, or
Micawber, or Bagstock, or Trabb's boy,—the thing
about each one of these persons is that he cannot be
exhausted. A Dickens character hits you first on the
nose and then in the waistcoat, and then in the eye and
then in the waistcoat again, with the blinding rapidity
of some battering engine. The scene in which Trabb's
boy continually overtakes Pip in order to reel and stagger as at a first encounter is a thing quite within
the real competence of such a character; it might have
been suggested by Thackeray, or George Eliot, or any
realist. But the point with Dickens is that there is a
rush in the boy's rushings; the writer and the reader
rush with him. They start with him, they stare with
him, they stagger with him, they share an inexpressible
vitality in the air which emanates from this violent and
capering satirist. Trabb's boy is among other things a
boy; he has a physical rapture in hurling himself like a
boomerang and in bouncing to the sky like a ball. It
is just exactly in describing this quality that Dickens is
Dickens and that no one else comes near him. No one
feels in his bones that Felix Holt was strong as he feels in
his bones that little Quilp was strong. No one can feel
that even Rawdon Crawley's splendid smack across the
face of Lord Steyne is quite so living and life-giving as
the "kick after kick" which old Mr. Weller dealt the
dancing and quivering Stiggins as he drove him towards
the trough. This quality, whether expressed intellec-

tually or physically, is the profoundly popular and eternal quality in Dickens; it is the thing that no one else could do.   This quality is the quality which has always given its continuous power and poetry to the common people everywhere.   It is life; it is the joy of life felt by those who have nothing else but life.   It is the thing that all aristocrats have always hated and dreaded in the people.   And it is the thing which poor Pip really hates and dreads in Trabb's boy.

A great man of letters or any great artist is symbolic without knowing it.   The things he describes are types because they are truths.   Shakespeare may, or may not, have ever put it to himself that Richard the Second was a philosophical symbol; but all good criticism must necessarily see him so.   It may be a reasonable question whether the artist should be allegorical.   There can be no doubt among sane men that the critic should be allegorical.   Spenser may have lost by being less realistic than Fielding.   But any good criticism of *Tom Jones* must be as mystical as the *Faery Queen*.   Hence it is unavoidable in speaking of a fine book like *Great Expectations* that we should give even to its unpretentious and realistic figures a certain massive mysticism.   Pip is Pip, but he is also the well-meaning snob.   And this is even more true of those two great figures in the tale which stand for the English democracy.   For, indeed, the first and last word upon the English democracy is said in Joe Gargery and Trabb's boy.   The actual English populace, as distinct from the French populace or the Scotch or Irish populace, may be said to lie between those two types.   The first is the poor man who does not assert himself at all, and the second is the poor man who asserts himself entirely with the weapon of sarcasm. The only way in which the English now ever rise in revolution is under the symbol and leadership of Trabb's boy. What pikes and shillelahs were to the Irish populace, what guns and barricades were to the French populace, that chaff is to the English populace. It is their weapon, the use of which they really understand. It is the one way in which they can make a rich man feel uncomfortable, and they use it very justifiably for all it is worth. If they do not cut off the heads of tyrants at least they sometimes do their best to make the tyrants lose their heads. The gutter boys of the great towns carry the art of personal criticism to so rich and delicate a degree that some well-dressed persons when they walk past a file of them feel as if they were walking past a row of omniscient critics or judges with a power of life and death. Here and there only is some ordinary human custom, some natural human pleasure suppressed in deference to the fastidiousness of the rich. But all the rich tremble before the fastidiousness of the poor.

Of the other type of democracy it is far more difficult to speak. It is always hard to speak of good things or good people, for in satisfying the soul they take away a certain spur to speech. Dickens was often called a sentimentalist. In one sense he sometimes was a sentimentalist. But if sentimentalism be held to mean something artificial or theatrical, then in the core and reality of his character Dickens was the very reverse of a sentimentalist. He seriously and definitely loved goodness. To see sincerity and charity satisfied

him like a meal. What some critics call his love of
sweet stuff is really his love of plain beef and bread.
Sometimes one is tempted to wish that in the long
Dickens dinner the sweet courses could be left out;
but this does not make the whole banquet other than
a banquet singularly solid and simple. The critics
complain of the sweet things, but not because they are
so strong as to like simple things. They complain of
the sweet things because they are so sophisticated as
to like sour things; their tongues are tainted with the
bitterness of absinthe. Yet because of the very simplicity of Dickens's moral tastes it is impossible to
speak adequately of them; and Joe Gargery must
stand as he stands in the book, a thing too obvious to
be understood. But this may be said of him in one
of his minor aspects, that he stands for a certain long-
suffering in the English poor, a certain weary patience
and politeness which almost breaks the heart. One
cannot help wondering whether that great mass of
silent virtue will ever achieve anything on this earth.

OUR MUTUAL FRIEND

Our Mutual Friend marks a happy return to the earlier manner of Dickens at the end of Dickens's life. One might call it a sort of Indian summer of his farce. Those who most truly love Dickens love the earlier Dickens; and any return to his farce must be welcomed, like a young man come back from the dead. In this book indeed he does not merely return to his farce; he returns in a manner to his vulgarity. It is the old democratic and even uneducated Dickens who is writing here. The very title is illiterate. Any priggish pupil teacher could tell Dickens that there is no such phrase in English as "our mutual friend." Any one could tell Dickens that "our mutual friend" means "our reciprocal friend," and that "our reciprocal friend" means nothing. If he had only had all the solemn advantages of academic learning (the absence of which in him was lamented by the *Quarterly Review*), he would have known better. He would have known that the correct phrase for a man known to two people is "our common friend." But if one calls one's friend a common friend, even that phrase is open to misunderstanding.

I dwell with a gloomy pleasure on this mistake in the very title of the book because I, for one, am not pleased to see Dickens gradually absorbed by modern culture and good manners. Dickens, by class and genius, belonged to the kind of people who do talk about a "mutual friend"; and for that class there is a very great deal to be said. These two things can at least be said—that this class does understand the meaning of the word "friend" and the meaning of the word "mutual." I know that for some long time before he had been slowly and subtly sucked into the whirlpool of the fashionable views of later England. I know that in *Bleak House* he treats the aristocracy far more tenderly than he treats them in *David Copperfield*. I know that in *A Tale of Two Cities*, having come under the influence of Carlyle, he treats revolution as strange and weird, whereas under the influence of Cobbett he would have treated it as obvious and reasonable. I know that in *The Mystery of Edwin Drood* he not only praised the Minor Canon of Cloisterham at the expense of the dissenting demagogue, Honeythunder; I know that he even took the last and most disastrous step in the modern English reaction. While blaming the old Cloisterham monks (who were democratic), he praised the old-world peace that they had left behind them—an old-world peace which is simply one of the last amusements of aristocracy. The modern rich feel quite at home with the dead monks. They would have felt anything but comfortable with the live ones. I know, in short, how the simple democracy of Dickens was gradually dimmed by the decay and reaction of the middle of the nineteenth century. I know that he fell into some of the bad habits of aristocratic sentimentalism. I know that he used the word "gentleman" as meaning good man. But all this only adds to the unholy joy with which I realise that the very title of one of his best books was a vulgarism. It is pleasant to contemplate this last unconscious knock in the eye for the gentility with which Dickens was half impressed. Dickens is the old self-made man; you may take him or leave him. He has its disadvantages and its merits. No university man would have written the title; no university man could have written the book.

If it were a mere matter of the accident of a name it would not be worth while thus to dwell on it, even as a preface. But the title is in this respect typical of the tale. The novel called *Our Mutual Friend* is in many ways a real reaction towards the earlier Dickens manner. I have remarked that *Little Dorrit* was a reversion to the form of the first books, but not to their spirit; *Our Mutual Friend* is a reversion to the spirit as well as the form. Compare, for instance, the public figures that make a background in each book. Mr. Merdle is a commercial man having no great connection with the plot; similarly Mr. Podsnap is a commercial man having no great connection with the plot. This is altogether in the spirit of the earlier books; the whole point of an early Dickens novel was to have as many people as possible entirely unconnected with the plot. But exactly because both studies are irrelevant, the contrast between them can be more clearly perceived. Dickens goes out of his way to describe Merdle; and it is a gloomy description. But Dickens goes out of his way to describe Podsnap, and it is a happy and hilarious description. It recalls the days when he hunted great game; when he went out of his way to entrap such adorable monsters as Mr. Pecksniff or Mr. Vincent Crummles. With these wild beings we never bother about the cause of their coming. Such guests in a story may be uninvited, but they are never *de trop*. They earn their night's lodging in any tale by being so uproariously amusing; like little Tommy Tucker in the legend, they sing for their supper. This is really the marked truth about *Our Mutual Friend*, as a stage in the singular latter career of Dickens. It is like the leaping up and flaming of a slowly dying fire. The best things in the book are in the old best manner of the author. They have that great Dickens quality of being something which is pure farce and yet which is not superficial; an unfathomable farce—a farce that goes down to the roots of the universe. The highest compliment that can ever be paid to the humour of Dickens is paid when some lady says, with the sudden sincerity of her sex, that it is "too silly." The phrase is really a perfectly sound and acute criticism. Humour does consist in being too silly, in passing the borderland, in breaking through the floor of sense and falling into some starry abyss of nonsense far below our ordinary human life. This "too silly" quality is really present in *Our Mutual Friend*. It is present in *Our Mutual Friend* just as it is present in *Pickwick*, or *Martin Chuzzlewit;* just as it is not present in *Little Dorrit* or in *Hard Times*. Many tests might be employed. One is the pleasure in purely physical jokes—jokes about the body. The general dislike which every one felt for Mr. Stiggins's nose is of the same kind as the ardent desire which Mr. Lammle felt for Mr. Fledgeby's nose. "Give me your nose, Sir," said Mr. Lammle. That sentence alone would be enough to show that the young Dickens had never died.

The opening of a book goes for a great deal. The

opening of *Our Mutual Friend* is much more instinctively energetic and light-hearted than that of any of
the other novels of his concluding period. Dickens had
always enough optimism to make his stories end well.
He had not, in his later years, always enough optimism
to make them begin well. Even *Great Expectations*,
the saddest of his later books, ends well; it ends well
in spite of himself, who had intended it to end badly.
But if we leave the evident case of good endings and
take the case of good beginnings, we see how much
Our Mutual Friend stands out from among the other
novels of the evening or the end of Dickens. The tale
of *Little Dorrit* begins in a prison. One of the prisoners
is a villain, and his villainy is as dreary as the prison;
that might matter nothing. But the other prisoner is
vivacious, and even his vivacity is dreary. The first
note struck is sad. In the tale of *Edwin Drood* the first
scene is in an opium den, suffocated with every sort of
phantasy and falsehood. Nor is it true that these
openings are merely accidental; they really cast their
shadow over the tales. The people of *Little Dorrit*
begin in prison; and it is the whole point of the book
that people never get out of prison. The story of
Edwin Drood begins amid the fumes of opium, and it
never gets out of the fumes of opium. The darkness of
that strange and horrible smoke is deliberately rolled
over the whole story. Dickens, in his later years,
permitted more and more his story to take the cue
from its inception. All the more remarkable, therefore,
is the real jerk and spurt of good spirits with which he
opens *Our Mutual Friend*. It begins with a good piece
of rowdy satire, wildly exaggerated and extremely true.

It belongs to the same class as the first chapter of *Martin Chuzzlewit*, with its preposterous pedigree of the Chuzzlewit family, or even the first chapter of *Pickwick*, with its immortal imbecilities about the Theory of Tittlebats and Mr. Blotton of Aldgate. Doubtless the early satiric chapter in *Our Mutual Friend* is of a more strategic and ingenious kind of satire than can be found in these early and explosive parodies. Still, there is a quality common to both, and that quality is the whole of Dickens. It is a quality difficult to define—hence the whole difficulty of criticising Dickens. Perhaps it can be best stated in two separate statements or as two separate symptoms. The first is the mere fact that the reader rushes to read it. The second is the mere fact that the writer rushed to write it.

This beginning, which is like a burst of the old exuberant Dickens, is, of course, the Veneering dinner-party. In its own way it is as good as anything that Dickens ever did. There is the old faculty of managing a crowd, of making character clash with character, that had made Dickens not only the democrat but even the demagogue of fiction. For if it is hard to manage a mob, it is hardest of all to manage a swell mob. The particular kind of chaos that is created by the hospitality of a rich upstart has perhaps never been so accurately and outrageously described. Every touch about the thing is true; to this day any one can test it if he goes to a dinner of this particular kind. How admirable, for instance, is the description of the way in which all the guests ignored the host; how the host and hostess peered and gaped for some stray attention as if they had been a pair of poor relations. Again, how well, as a matter

of social colour, the distinctions between the type and
tone of the guests are made even in the matter of this
unguestlike insolence. How well Dickens distinguishes
the ill-bred indifference of Podsnap from the well-bred
indifference of Mortimer Lightwood and Eugene Wray-
burn. How well he distinguishes the bad manners of
the merchant from the equally typical bad manners of
the gentleman. Above all, how well he catches the
character of the creature who is really the master of all
these: the impenetrable male servant. Nowhere in
literature is the truth about servants better told.
For that truth is simply this: that the secret of aristocracy is hidden even from aristocrats. Servants, butlers,
footmen, are the high priests who have the real dis-
pensation; and even gentlemen are afraid of them.
Dickens was never more right than when he made the
new people, the Veneerings, employ a butler who despised
not only them but all their guests and acquaintances.
The admirable person called the Analytical Chemist
shows his perfection particularly in the fact that he regards all the sham gentlemen and all the real gentlemen
with the same gloomy and incurable contempt. He
offers wine to the offensive Podsnap or the shrieking
Tippins with a melancholy sincerity and silence; but
he offers his letter to the aristocratic and unconscious
Mortimer with the same sincerity and with the same
silence. It is a great pity that the Analytical Chemist
only occurs in two or three scenes of this excellent story.
As far as I know, he never really says a word from one
end of the book to the other; but he is one of the best
characters in Dickens.

Round the Veneering dinner-table are collected not

indeed the best characters in Dickens, but certainly
the best characters in *Our Mutual Friend*. Certainly
one exception must be made. Fledgeby is unaccount-
ably absent. There was really no reason why he should
not have been present at a dinner-party given by the
Veneerings and including the Lammles. His money
was at least more genuine than theirs. If he had been
present the party would really have included all that
is important in *Our Mutual Friend*. For indeed, outside Mr. Fledgeby and the people at the dinner-party,
there is something a little heavy and careless about the
story. Mr. Silas Wegg is really funny; and he serves
the purpose of a necessary villain in the plot. But his
humour and his villainy seem to have no particular connection with each other; when he is not scheming he
seems the last man likely to scheme. He is rather like
one of Dickens's agreeable Bohemians, a pleasant com-
panion, a quoter of fine verses. His villainy seems an
artificial thing attached to him, like his wooden leg.
For while his villainy is supposed to be of a dull, mean,
and bitter sort (quite unlike, for instance, the uproarious
villainy of Quilp), his humour is of the sincere, flowing
and lyric character, like that of Dick Swiveller or Mr.
Micawber. He tells Mr. Boffin that he will drop into
poetry in a friendly way. He does drop into it in a
friendly way; in much too really a friendly way to make
him convincing as a mere calculating knave. He and
Mr. Venus are such natural and genuine companions
that one does not see why if Venus repents Wegg should
not repent too. In short, Wegg is a convenience for a
plot and not a very good plot at that. But if he is
one of the blots on the business, he is not the principal

one. If the real degradation of Wegg is not very convincing, it is at least immeasurably more convincing than the pretended degradation of Boffin. The passage in which Boffin appears as a sort of miser, and then afterwards explains that he only assumed the character for reasons of his own, has something about it highly jerky and unsatisfactory. The truth of the whole matter I think, almost certainly, is that Dickens did not originally mean Boffin's lapse to be fictitious. He originally meant Boffin really to be corrupted by wealth, slowly to degenerate and as slowly to repent. But the story went too quickly for this long, double, and difficult process; therefore Dickens at the last moment made a sudden recovery possible by representing that the whole business had been a trick. Consequently, this episode is not an error merely in the sense that we may find many errors in a great writer like Dickens; it is a mistake patched up with another mistake. It is a case of that ossification which occurs round the healing of an actual fracture; the story had broken down and been mended.

If Dickens had fulfilled what was probably his original design, and described the slow freezing of Boffin's soul in prosperity, I do not say that he would have done the thing well. He was not good at describing change in anybody, especially not good at describing a change for the worse. The tendency of all his characters is upwards, like bubbles, never downwards, like stones. But at least it would probably have been more credible than the story as it stands; for the story as it stands is actually less credible than any conceivable kind of moral ruin for Boffin. Such a character as his—rough, simple and lumberingly unconscious—might be more

easily conceived as really sinking in self-respect and
honour than as keeping up, month after month, so
strained and inhuman a theatrical performance.   To a
good man (of that particular type) it would be easier
to be bad than to pretend to be bad.   It might have
taken years to turn Noddy Boffin into a miser; but it
would have taken centuries to turn him into an actor.
This unreality in the later Boffin scenes makes the end
of the story of John Harmon somewhat more unimpressive perhaps than it might otherwise have been.
Upon no hypothesis, however, can he be made one of
the more impressive figures of Dickens.   It is true that
it is an unfair criticism to object, as some have done,
that Dickens does not succeed in disguising the identity
of John Harmon with John Rokesmith.   Dickens
never intended to disguise it; the whole story would be
mainly unintelligible and largely uninteresting if it had
been successfully disguised.   But though John Harmon
or Rokesmith was never intended to be merely a man of
mystery, it is not quite so easy to say what he was
intended to be.   Bella is a possible and pretty sketch.
Mrs. Wilfer, her mother, is an entirely impossible and
entirely delightful one.   Miss Podsnap is not only excellent, she is to a healthy taste positively attractive;
there is a real suggestion in her of the fact that humility
is akin to truth, even when humility takes its more
comic form of shyness.   There is not in all literature a
more human *cri de cœur* than that with which Georgiana
Podsnap receives the information that a young man
has professed himself to be attracted by her—"Oh
what a Fool he must be!"

Two other figures require praise, though they are in

the more tragic manner which Dickens touched from time to time in his later period. Bradley Headstone is really a successful villain; so successful that he fully captures our sympathies. Also there is something original in the very conception. It was a new notion to add to the villains of fiction, whose thoughts go quickly, this villain whose thoughts go slow but sure; and it was a new notion to combine a deadly criminality not with high life or the slums (the usual haunts for villains) but with the laborious respectability of the lower, middle classes. The other good conception is the boy, Bradley Headstone's pupil, with his dull, inexhaustible egoism, his pert, unconscious cruelty, and the strict decorum and incredible baseness of his views of life. It is singular that Dickens, who was not only a radical and a social reformer, but one who would have been particularly concerned to maintain the principle of modern popular education, should nevertheless have seen so clearly this potential evil in the mere education-alism of our time—the fact that merely educating the democracy may easily mean setting to work to despoil it of all the democratic virtues. It is better to be Lizzie Hexam and not know how to read and write than to be Charlie Hexam and not know how to appreciate Lizzie Hexam. It is not only necessary that the democracy should be taught; it is also necessary that the democracy should be taught democracy. Otherwise it will certainly fall a victim to that snobbishness and system of worldly standards which is the most natural and easy of all the forms of human corruption. This is one of the many dangers which Dickens saw before it existed. Dickens was really a prophet; far more of a prophet than Carlyle.

EDWIN DROOD

Pickwick was a work partly designed by others, but
ultimately filled up by Dickens. *Edwin Drood*, the
last book, was a book designed by Dickens, but ultimately filled up by others. The *Pickwick Papers*
showed how much Dickens could make out of other
people's suggestions; *The Mystery of Edwin Drood*
shows how very little other people can make out of
Dickens's suggestions.

Dickens was meant by Heaven to be the great melo-
dramatist; so that even his literary end was melodramatic. Something more seems hinted at in the cutting short
of *Edwin Drood* by Dickens than the mere cutting short
of a good novel by a great man. It seems rather like
the last taunt of some elf, leaving the world, that it
should be this story which is not ended, this story which
is only a story. The only one of Dickens's novels
which he did not finish was the only one that really
needed finishing. He never had but one thoroughly
good plot to tell; and that he has only told in heaven.
This is what separates the case in question from any
parallel cases of novelists cut off in the act of creation.
That great novelist, for instance, with whom Dickens
is constantly compared, died also in the middle of
Denis Duval. But any one can see in *Denis Duval*
the qualities of the later work of Thackeray; the

increasing discursiveness, the increasing retrospective
poetry, which had been in part the charm and in part
the failure of *Philip* and *The Virginians*. But to
Dickens it was permitted to die at a dramatic moment
and to leave a dramatic mystery. Any Thackerayan
could have completed the plot of *Denis Duval;* except
indeed that a really sympathetic Thackerayan might
have had some doubt as to whether there was any plot
to complete. But Dickens, having had far too little
plot in his stories previously, had far too much plot
in the story he never told. Dickens dies in the act of
telling, not his tenth novel, but his first news of murder.
He drops down dead as he is in the act of denouncing
the assassin. It is permitted to Dickens, in short, to
come to a literary end as strange as his literary beginning. He began by completing the old romance of
travel. He ended by inventing the new detective story.

It is as a detective story first and last that we have
to consider *The Mystery of Edwin Drood*. This does not
mean, of course, that the details are not often admirable
in their swift and penetrating humour; to say that of
the book would be to say that Dickens did not write it.
Nothing could be truer, for instance, than the manner
in which the dazed and drunken dignity of Durdles
illustrates a certain bitterness at the bottom of the
bewilderment of the poor. Nothing could be better
than the way in which the haughty and allusive conversation between Miss Twinkleton and the landlady
illustrates the maddening preference of some females
for skating upon thin social ice. There is an even
better example than these of the original humorous
insight of Dickens; and one not very often remarked,

because of its brevity and its unimportance in the
narrative. But Dickens never did anything better
than the short account of Mr. Grewgious's dinner being
brought from the tavern by two waiters: "a stationary
waiter," and "a flying waiter." The "flying waiter"
brought the food and the "stationary waiter" quarrelled
with him; the "flying waiter" brought glasses and the
"stationary waiter" looked through them. Finally, it
will be remembered the "stationary waiter" left the
room, casting a glance which indicated "let it be understood that all emoluments are mine, and that Nil is
the reward of this slave." Still, Dickens wrote the
book as a detective story; he wrote it as *The Mystery
of Edwin Drood*. And alone, perhaps, among detective-
story writers, he never lived to destroy his mystery.
Here alone then among the Dickens novels it is necessary to speak of the plot and of the plot alone. And
when we speak of the plot it becomes immediately
necessary to speak of the two or three standing explanations which celebrated critics have given of the plot.

The story, so far as it was written by Dickens, can
be read here. It describes, as will be seen, the disappearance of the young architect Edwin Drood after
a night of festivity which was supposed to celebrate his
reconciliation with a temporary enemy, Neville Landless, and was held at the house of his uncle John Jasper.
Dickens continued the tale long enough to explain or
explode the first and most obvious of his riddles.
Long before the existing part terminates it has become
evident that Drood has been put away, not by his
obvious opponent, Landless, but by his uncle who professes for him an almost painful affection. The fact

that we all know this, however, ought not in fairness to blind us to the fact that, considered as the first fraud in a detective story, it has been, with great skill, at once suggested and concealed. Nothing, for instance, could be cleverer as a piece of artistic mystery than the fact that Jasper, the uncle, always kept his eyes fixed on Drood's face with a dark and watchful tenderness; the thing is so told that at first we really take it as only indicating something morbid in the affection; it is only afterwards that the frightful fancy breaks upon us that it is not morbid affection but morbid antagonism. This first mystery (which is no longer a mystery) of Jasper's guilt, is only worth remarking because it shows that Dickens meant and felt himself able to mask all his batteries with real artistic strategy and artistic caution. The manner of the unmasking of Jasper marks the manner and tone in which the whole tale was to be told. Here we have not got to do with Dickens simply giving himself away, as he gave himself away in *Pickwick* or *The Christmas Carol*. Not that one complains of his giving himself away; there was no better gift.

What was the mystery of Edwin Drood from Dickens's point of view we shall never know, except perhaps from Dickens in heaven, and then he will very likely have forgotten. But the mystery of Edwin Drood from our point of view, from that of his critics, and those who have with some courage (after his death) attempted to be his collaborators, is simply this. There is no doubt that Jasper either murdered Drood or supposed that he had murdered him. This certainty we have from the fact that it is the whole point of a scene between Jasper and Drood's lawyer Grewgious

in which Jasper is struck down with remorse when he
realises that Drood has been killed (from his point
of view) needlessly and without profit. The only
question is whether Jasper's remorse was as needless as
his murder.   In other words the only question is
whether, while he certainly thought he had murdered
Drood, he had really done it.   It need hardly be said
that such a doubt would not have been raised for nothing; gentlemen like Jasper do not as a rule waste good
remorse except upon successful crime.   The origin of
the doubt about the real death of Drood is this.   Towards the latter end of the existing chapters there
appears very abruptly, and with a quite ostentatious
air of mystery, a character called Datchery.   He
appears for the purpose of spying upon Jasper and
getting up some case against him; at any rate, if
he has not this purpose in the story he has no other
earthly purpose in it.   He is an old gentleman of juve-
nile energy, with a habit of carrying his hat in his
hand even in the open air; which some have interpreted
as meaning that he feels the unaccustomed weight of a
wig.   Now there are one or two people in the story who
this person might possibly be.   Notably there is one
person in the story who seems as if he were meant to be
something, but who hitherto has certainly been nothing;
I mean Bazzard, Mr. Grewgious's clerk, a sulky fellow
interested in theatricals, of whom an unnecessary fuss
is made.   There is also Mr. Grewgious himself, and
there is also another suggestion, so much more startling
that I shall have to deal with it later.

For the moment, however, the point is this: That
ingenious writer, Mr. Proctor, started the highly

plausible theory that this Datchery was Drood himself, who had not really been killed. He adduced a most complex and complete scheme covering nearly all the details; but the strongest argument he had was rather one of general artistic effect. This argument has been quite perfectly summed up by Mr. Andrew Lang in one sentence: "If Edwin Drood is dead, there is not much mystery about him." This is quite true; Dickens, when writing in so deliberate, nay, dark and conspiratorial a manner, would surely have kept the death of Drood and the guilt of Jasper hidden a little longer if the only real mystery had been the guilt of Jasper and the death of Drood. It certainly seems artistically more likely that there was a further mystery of Edwin Drood; not the mystery that he was murdered, but the mystery that he was not murdered. It is true indeed that Mr. Cumming Walters has a theory of Datchery (to which I have already darkly alluded) a theory which is wild enough to be the centre not only of any novel but of any harlequinade. But the point is that even Mr. Cumming Walters's theory, though it makes the mystery more extraordinary, does not make it any more of a mystery of Edwin Drood. It should not have been called *The Mystery of Drood*, but *The Mystery of Datchery*. This is the strongest case for Proctor; if the story tells of Drood coming back as Datchery, the story does at any rate fulfil the title upon its title-page.

The principal objection to Proctor's theory is that there seems no adequate reason why Jasper should not have murdered his nephew if he wanted to. And there seems even less reason why Drood, if unsuccessfully murdered, should not have raised the alarm. Happy young architects, when nearly strangled by elderly organists, do not generally stroll away and come back some time afterwards in a wig and with a false name. Superficially it would seem almost as odd to find the murderer investigating the origin of the murder, as to find the corpse investigating it.   To this problem two of the ablest literary critics of our time, Mr. Andrew Lang and Mr. William Archer (both of them persuaded generally of the Proctor theory) have especially addressed themselves.   Both have come to the same substantial conclusion; and I suspect that they are right.   They hold that Jasper (whose mania for opium is much insisted on in the tale) had some sort of fit, or trance, or other physical seizure as he was committing the crime so that he left it unfinished; and they also hold that he had drugged Drood, so that Drood, when he recovered from the attack, was doubtful about who had been his assailant.   This might really explain, if a little fancifully, his coming back to the town in the character of a detective.   He might think it due to his uncle (whom he last remembered in a kind of murderous vision) to make an independent investigation as to whether he was really guilty or not.   He might say, as Hamlet said of a vision equally terrifying, "I 'll have grounds more relative than this."   In fairness it must be said that there is something vaguely shaky about this theory; chiefly, I think, in this respect; that there is a sort of farcical cheerfulness about Datchery which does not seem altogether appropriate to a lad who ought to be in an agony of doubt as to whether his best friend was or was not his assassin.   Still there are many such incongruities in Dickens; and the explanation of Mr. Archer and Mr. Lang is an explanation. I do not believe that any explanation as good can be given to account for the tale being called *The Mystery of Edwin Drood*, if the tale practically starts with his corpse.

If Drood is really dead one cannot help feeling the story ought to end where it does end, not by accident but by design. The murder is explained. Jasper is ready to be hanged, and every one else in a decent novel ought to be ready to be married. If there was to be much more of anything, it must have been of anti-climax. Nevertheless there are degrees of anti-climax. Some of the more obvious explanations of Datchery are quite reasonable, but they are distinctly tame. For instance, Datchery may be Bazzard; but it is not very exciting if he is; for we know nothing about Bazzard and care less. Again, he might be Grewgious; but there is something pointless about one grotesque character dressing up as another grotesque character actually less amusing than himself. Now, Mr. Cumming Walters has at least had the distinction of inventing a theory which makes the story at least an interesting story, even if it is not exactly the story that is promised on the cover of the book. The obvious enemy of Drood, on whom suspicion first falls, the swarthy and sulky Landless, has a sister even swarthier and, except for her queenly dignity, even sulkier than he. This barbaric princess is evidently meant to be (in a sombre way) in love with Crisparkle, the clergyman and muscular Christian who represents the breezy element in the emotions of the tale. Mr. Cumming Walters seriously maintains that it is this barbaric princess who puts on a wig and dresses up as Mr. Datchery. He urges his case with much ingenuity of detail. Helena Landless certainly had a motive; to save her brother, who was accused falsely, by accusing Jasper justly. She certainly had some of the faculties; it is elaborately stated in the earlier part of her story that she was accustomed as a child to dress up in male costume and run into the wildest adventures. There may be something in Mr. Cumming Walters's argument that the very flippancy of Datchery is the self-conscious flippancy of a strong woman in such an odd situation; certainly there is the same flippancy in Portia and in Rosalind. Nevertheless, I think, there is one final objection to the theory; and that is simply this, that it is comic. It is generally wrong to represent a great master of the grotesque as being grotesque exactly where he does not intend to be. And I am persuaded that if Dickens had really meant Helena to turn into Datchery, he would have made her from the first in some way more light, eccentric, and laughable; he would have made her at least as light and laughable as Rosa. As it is, there is something strangely stiff and incredible about the idea of a lady so dark and dignified dressing up as a swaggering old gentleman in a blue coat and grey trousers. We might almost as easily imagine Edith Dombey dressing up as Major Bagstock. We might almost as easily imagine Rebecca in *Ivanhoe* dressing up as Isaac of York.

Of course such a question can never really be settled precisely, because it is the question not merely of a mystery but of a puzzle. For here the detective novel differs from every other kind of novel. The ordinary novelist desires to keep his readers to the point; the detective novelist actually desires to keep his readers off the point. In the first case, every touch must help to tell the reader what he means; in the second case, most of the touches must conceal or even contradict what he means. You are supposed to see and appreciate the smallest gestures of a good actor; but you do not see all the gestures of a conjuror, if he is a good conjuror. Hence, into the critical estimate of such works as this, there is introduced a problem, an extra perplexity, which does not exist in other cases. I mean the˜problem of the things commonly called blinds. Some of the points which we pick out as suggestive may have been put in as deceptive. Thus the whole conflict between a critic with one theory, like Mr. Lang, and a critic with another theory, like Mr. Cumming Walters, becomes eternal and a trifle farcical. Mr. Walters says that all Mr. Lang's clues were blinds; Mr. Lang says that all Mr. Walters's clues were blinds. Mr. Walters can say that some passages seemed to show that Helena was Datchery; Mr. Lang can reply that those passages were only meant to deceive simple people like Mr. Walters into supposing that she was Datchery. Similarly Mr. Lang can say that the return of Drood is foreshadowed; and Mr. Walters can reply that it was foreshadowed because it was never meant to come off. There seems no end to this insane process; anything that Dickens wrote may or may not mean the opposite of what it says. Upon this principle I should be very ready for one to declare that all the suggested Datcherys were really blinds; merely because they can naturally be suggested. I would undertake to maintain that Mr.

Datchery is really Miss Twinkleton, who has a mercenary interest in keeping Rosa Budd at her school. This suggestion does not seem to me to be really much more humorous than Mr. Cumming Walters's theory. Yet either may certainly be true. Dickens is dead, and a number of splendid scenes and startling adventures have died with him. Even if we get the right solution we shall not know that it is right. The tale might have been, and yet it has not been.

And I think there is no thought so much calculated to make one doubt death itself, to feel that sublime doubt which has created all religion—the doubt that found death incredible. Edwin Drood may or may not have really died; but surely Dickens did not really die. Surely our real detective liveth and shall appear in the latter days of the earth. For a finished tale may give a man immortality in the light and literary sense; but an unfinished tale suggests another immortality, more essential and more strange.

MASTER HUMPHREY'S CLOCK

IT is quite indispensable to include a criticism of *Master Humphrey's Clock* in any survey of Dickens, although it is not one of the books of which his admirers would chiefly boast; although perhaps it is almost the only one of which he would not have boasted himself. As a triumph of Dickens, at least, it is not of great importance. But as a sample of Dickens it happens to be of quite remarkable importance. The very fact that it is for the most part somewhat more level and even monotonous than most of his creations, makes us realise, as it were, against what level and monotony those creations commonly stand out. This book is the background of his mind. It is the basis and minimum of him which was always there. Alone, of all written things, this shows how he felt when he was not writing. Dickens might have written it in his sleep. That is to say, it is written by a sluggish Dickens, a half automatic Dickens, a dreaming and drifting Dickens; but still by the enduring Dickens.

But this truth can only be made evident by beginning nearer to the root of the matter. *Nicholas Nickleby* had just completed, or, to speak more strictly, confirmed, the popularity of the young author; wonderful as *Pickwick* was it might have been a nine days' wonder; *Oliver Twist* had been powerful but painful; it was

Nicholas Nickleby that proved the man to be a great productive force of which one could ask more, of which one could ask all things. His publishers, Chapman and Hall, seem to have taken at about this point that step which sooner or later most publishers do take with regard to a half successful man who is becoming wholly successful. Instead of asking him for something, they asked him for anything. They made him, so to speak, the editor of his own works. And indeed it is literally as the editor of his own works that he next appears; for the next thing to which he proposes to put his name is not a novel, but for all practical purposes a magazine. Yet although it is a magazine, it is a magazine entirely written by himself; the publishers, in point of fact, wanted to create a kind of Dickens Miscellany, in a much more literal sense than that in which we speak of a Bentley Miscellany. Dickens was in no way disposed to dislike such a job; for the more miscellaneous he was the more he enjoyed himself. And indeed this early experiment of his bears a great deal of resemblance to those later experiences in which he was the editor of two popular periodicals. The editor of *Master Humphrey's Clock* was a kind of type or precursor of the editor of *Household Words* and *All the Year Round*. There was the same sense of absolute ease in an atmosphere of infinite gossip. There was the same great advantage gained by a man of genius who wrote best scrappily and by episodes. The omnipotence of the editor helped the eccentricities of the author. He could excuse himself for all his own shortcomings. He could begin a novel, get tired of it, and turn it into a short story. He could begin a short

story, get fond of it, and turn it into a novel.   Thus in
the days of *Household Words* he could begin a big
scheme of stories, such as *Somebody's Luggage*, or
Seven Poor Travellers, and after writing a tale or two
toss the rest to his colleagues.   Thus, on the other
hand, in the time of *Master Humphrey's Clock*, he
could begin one small adventure of Master Humphrey
and find himself unable to stop it.   It is quite clear I
think (though only from moral evidence, which some
call reading between the lines) that he originally meant
to tell many separate tales of Master Humphrey's
wanderings in London, only one of which, and that
a short one, was to have been concerned with a little
girl going home.   Fortunately for us that little girl
had a grandfather, and that grandfather had a curiosity
shop and also a nephew, and that nephew had an
entirely irrelevant friend whom men and angels called
Richard Swiveller.   Once having come into the society
of Swiveller it is not unnatural that Dickens stayed
there for a whole book.   The essential point for us
here, however, is that *Master Humphrey's Clock* was
stopped by the size and energy of the thing that had
come of it.   It died in childbirth.

There is, however, another circumstance which,
even in ordinary public opinion, makes this miscellany
important, besides the great novel that came out of it.
I mean that the ordinary reader can remember one
great thing about *Master Humphrey's Clock*, besides
the fact that it was the frame-work of *The Old Curiosity
Shop*.   He remembers that Mr. Pickwick and the
Wellers rise again from the dead.   Dickens makes
Samuel Pickwick become a member of Master Hum-

phrey's Clock Society; and he institutes a parallel
society in the kitchen under the name of Mr. Weller's
Watch.

Before we consider the question of whether Dickens
was wise when he did this, it is worth remarking how
really odd it is that this is the only place where he did it.
Dickens, one would have thought, was the one man
who might naturally have introduced old characters
into new stories.   Dickens, as a matter of fact, was
almost the one man who never did it.   It would have
seemed natural in him for a double reason; first, that
his characters were very valuable to him, and second
that they were not very valuable to his particular
stories.   They were dear to him, and they are dear to
us; but they really might as well have turned up
(within reason) in one environment as well as in another.
We, I am sure, should be delighted to meet Mr. Mantalini in the story of *Dombey and Son*.   And he certainly would not be much missed from the plot of
Nicholas Nickleby.   "I am an affectionate father,"
said Dickens, "to all the children of my fancy; but like
many other parents I have in my heart of hearts a
favourite child; and his name is David Copperfield."
Yet although his heart must often have yearned backwards to the children of his fancy whose tale was already told, yet he never touched one of them again
even with the point of his pen.   The characters in
David Copperfield, as in all the others, were dead for
him after he had done the book; if he loved them as
children, it was as dead and sanctified children.   It is
a curious test of the strength and even reticence that
underlay the seeming exuberance of Dickens, that he

never did yield at all to exactly that indiscretion or act of sentimentalism which would seem most natural to his emotions and his art. Or rather he never did yield to it except here in this one case; the case of *Master Humphrey's Clock*.

And it must be remembered that nearly everybody else did yield to it. Especially did those writers who are commonly counted Dickens's superiors in art and exactitude and closeness to connected reality. Thackeray wallowed in it; Anthony Trollope lived on it. Those modern artists who pride themselves most on the separation and unity of a work of art have indulged in it often; thus, for instance, Stevenson gave a glimpse of Alan Breck in *The Master of Ballantrae*, and meant to give a glimpse of the Master of Ballantrae in another unwritten tale called *The Rising Sun*. The habit of revising old characters is so strong in Thackeray that *Vanity Fair, Pendennis, The Newcomes*, and *Philip* are in one sense all one novel. Certainly the reader sometimes forgets which one of them he is reading. Afterwards he cannot remember whether the best description of Lord Steyne's red whiskers or Mr. Wagg's rude jokes occurred in *Vanity Fair*, or *Pendennis;* he cannot remember whether his favourite dialogue between Mr. and Mrs. Pendennis occurred in *The Newcomes*, or in *Philip*. Whenever two Thackeray characters in two Thackeray novels could by any possibility have been contemporary, Thackeray delights to connect them. He makes Major Pendennis nod to Dr. Firmin, and Colonel Newcome ask Major Dobbin to dinner. Whenever two characters could not possibly have been contemporary he goes out of his

way to make one the remote ancestor of the other.
Thus he created the great house of Warrington solely
to connect a "blue-bearded" Bohemian journalist
with the blood of Henry Esmond. It is quite impossible to conceive Dickens keeping up this elaborate
connection between all his characters and all his books,
especially across the ages. It would give us a kind of
shock if we learnt from Dickens that Major Bagstock
was the nephew of Mr. Chester. Still less can we
imagine Dickens carrying on an almost systematic
family chronicle as was in some sense done by Trollope.
There must be some reason for such a paradox; for in
itself it is a very curious one. The writers who wrote
carefully were always putting, as it were, after-words
and appendices to their already finished portraits;
the man who did splendid and flamboyant but faulty
portraits never attempted to touch them up. Or
rather (we may say again) he attempted it once, and
then he failed.

The reason lay, I think, in the very genius of
Dickens's creation. The child he bore of his soul
quitted him when his term was passed like a verit-
able child born of the body. It was independent of
him, as a child is of its parents. It had become dead
to him even in becoming alive. When Thackeray
studied Pendennis or Lord Steyne he was studying
something outside himself, and therefore something
that might come nearer and nearer. But when Dickens
brought forth Sam Weller or Pickwick he was creating
something that had once been inside himself and therefore when once created could only go further and further
away. It may seem a strange thing to say of such

laughable characters and of so lively an author, yet I say it quite seriously; I think it possible that there arose between Dickens and his characters that strange and almost supernatural shyness that arises often between parents and children; because they are too close to each other to be open with each other. Too much hot and high emotion had gone to the creation of one of his great figures for it to be possible for him without embarrassment ever to speak with it again. This is the thing which some fools call fickleness; but which is not the death of feeling, but rather its dreadful perpetuation; this shyness is the final seal of strong sentiment; this coldness is an eternal constancy.

This one case where Dickens broke through his rule was not such a success as to tempt him in any case to try the thing again.

There is weakness in the strict sense of the word in this particular reappearance of Samuel Pickwick and Samuel Weller. In the original *Pickwick Papers* Dickens had with quite remarkable delicacy and vividness contrived to suggest a certain fundamental sturdiness and spirit in that corpulent and complacent old gentleman. Mr. Pickwick was a mild man, a respectable man, a placid man; but he was very decidedly a man. He could denounce his enemies and fight for his nightcap. He was fat; but he had a backbone. In *Master Humphrey's Clock* the backbone seems somehow to be broken; his good nature seems limp instead of alert. He gushes out of his good heart; instead of taking a good heart for granted as a part of any decent gentleman's furniture as did the older and stronger Pickwick. The truth is, I think, that Mr. Pickwick

in complete repose loses some part of the whole point
of his existence. The quality which makes the *Pickwick Papers* one of the greatest of human fairy tales
is a quality which all the great fairy tales possess, and
which marks them out from most modern writing.   A
modern novelist generally endeavours to make his
story interesting, by making his hero odd.   The most
typical modern books are those in which the central
figure is himself or herself an exception, a cripple, a
courtesan, a lunatic, a swindler, or a person of the most
perverse temperament.   Such stories, for instance,
are *Sir Richard Calmady*, *Dodo*, *Quisante*, *La Bête
Humaine*, even the *Egoist*.   But in a fairy tale the boy
sees all the wonders of fairyland because he is an ordinary boy.   In the same way Mr. Samuel Pickwick
sees an extraordinary England because he is an ordinary
old gentleman.   He does not see things through the
rosy spectacles of the modern optimist or the green-
smoked spectacles of the pessimist; he sees it through
the crystal glasses of his own innocence.   One must
see the world clearly even in order to see its wildest
poetry.   One must see it sanely even in order to see
that it is insane.

Mr. Pickwick, then, relieved against a background of
heavy kindliness and quiet club life does not seem to be
quite the same heroic figure as Mr. Pickwick relieved
against a background of the fighting police constables at
Ipswich or the roaring mobs of Eatanswill.   Of the
degeneration of the Wellers, though it has been commonly assumed by critics, I am not so sure.   Some of
the things said in the humorous assembly round Mr.
Weller's Watch are really human and laughable and

altogether in the old manner. Especially, I think, the vague and awful allusiveness of old Mr. Weller when he reminds his little grandson of his delinquencies under the trope or figure of their being those of another little boy, is really in the style both of the irony and the domesticity of the poorer classes. Sam also says one or two things really worthy of himself. We feel almost as if Sam were a living man, and could not appear for an instant without being amusing.

The other elements in the make-up of *Master Humphrey's Clock* come under the same paradox which I have applied to the whole work. Though not very important in literature they are somehow quite important in criticism. They show us better than anything else the whole unconscious trend of Dickens, the stuff of which his very dreams were made. If he had made up tales to amuse himself when half-awake (as I have no doubt he did) they would be just such tales as these. They would have been ghostly legends of the nooks and holes of London, echoes of old love and laughter from the taverns or the Inns of Court. In a sense also one may say that these tales are the great might-have-beens of Dickens. They are chiefly designs which he fills up here slightly and unsatisfactorily, but which he might have filled up with his own brightest and most incredible colours. Nothing, for instance, could have been nearer to the heart of Dickens than his great Gargantuan conception of Gog and Magog telling London legends to each other all through the night. Those two giants might have stood on either side of some new great city of his invention, swarming with fanciful figures and noisy with new events. But as it is, the two giants stand alone in a wilderness, guarding either side of a gate that leads nowhere.

REPRINTED PIECES

THOSE abuses which are supposed to belong specially
to religion belong to all human institutions. They
are not the sins of supernaturalism, but the sins of
nature. In this respect it is interesting to observe
that all the evils which our Rationalist or Protestant
tradition associates with the idolatrous veneration of
sacred figures arises in the merely human atmosphere
of literature and history. Every extravagance of
hagiology can be found in hero-worship. Every folly
alleged in the worship of saints can be found in the
worship of poets. There are those who are honourably
and intensely opposed to the atmosphere of religious
symbolism or religious archæology. There are people
who have a vague idea that the worship of saints is
worse than the imitation of sinners. There are some,
like a lady I once knew, who think that hagiology
is the scientific study of hags. But these slightly
prejudiced persons generally have idolatries and superstitions of their own, particularly idolatries and superstitions in connection with celebrated people. Mr.
Stead preserves a pistol belonging to Oliver Cromwell
in the office of the *Review of Reviews;* and I am sure he
worships it in his rare moments of solitude and leisure.
A man, who could not be induced to believe in God

by all the arguments of all the philosophers, professed himself ready to believe if he could see it stated on a postcard in the handwriting of Mr. Gladstone. Persons not otherwise noted for their religious exercise have been known to procure and preserve portions of the hair of Paderewski. Nay, by this time blasphemy itself is a sacred tradition, and almost as much respect would be paid to the alleged relics of an atheist as to the alleged relics of a god. .If any one has a fork that belonged to Voltaire, he could probably exchange it in the open market for a knife that belonged to St. Theresa.

Of all the instances of this there is none stranger than the case of Dickens. It should be pondered very carefully by those who reproach Christianity with having been easily corrupted into a system of superstitions. If ever there was a message full of what modern people call true Christianity, the direct appeal to the common heart, a faith that was simple, a hope that was infinite, and a charity that was omnivorous, if ever there came among men what they call the Christianity of Christ, it was in the message of Dickens. Christianity has been in the world nearly two thousand years, and it has not yet quite lost, its enemies being judges, its first fire and charity; but friends and enemies would agree that it was from the very first more detailed and doctrinal than the spirit of Dickens. The spirit of Dickens has been in the world about sixty years; and already it is a superstition. Already it is loaded with relics. Already it is stiff with antiquity.

Everything that can be said about the perversion of Christianity can be said about the perversion of

Dickens. It is said that Christ's words are repeated
by the very High Priests and Scribes whom He meant to
denounce. It is just as true that the jokes in *Pickwick*
are quoted with delight by the very bigwigs of bench
and bar whom Dickens wished to make absurd and
impossible. It is said that texts from Scripture are
constantly taken in vain by Judas and Herod, by
Caiaphas and Annas. It is just as true that texts from
Dickens are rapturously quoted on all our platforms
by Podsnap and Honeythunder, by Pardiggle and
Veneering, by Tigg when he is forming a company, or
Pott when he is founding a newspaper. People joke
about Bumble in defence of Bumbledom; people allude
playfully to Mrs. Jellyby while agitating for Borrio-
boola Gha. The very things which Dickens tried to destroy are preserved as relics of him. The very houses
he wished to pull down are propped up as monuments
of Dickens. We wish to preserve everything of him,
except his perilous public spirit.

This antiquarian attitude towards Dickens has many
manifestations, some of them somewhat ridiculous. I
give one startling instance out of a hundred of the
irony remarked upon above. In his first important
book, Dickens lashed the loathsome corruption of our
oligarchical politics, their blaring servility and dirty
diplomacy of bribes, under the name of an imaginary
town called Eatanswill. If Eatanswill, wherever it
was, had been burned to the ground by its indignant
neighbours the day after the exposure, it would have
been not inappropriate. If it had been entirely
deserted by its inhabitants, if they had fled to hide
themselves in holes and caverns, one could have un-

derstood it.   If it had been struck by a thunderbolt out
of heaven or outlawed by the whole human race, all that
would seem quite natural.   What has really happened
is this: that two respectable towns in Suffolk are still
disputing for the honour of having been the original
Eatanswill; as if two innocent hamlets each claimed to
be Gomorrah.   I make no comment; the thing is beyond speech.

But this strange sentimental and relic-hunting worship of Dickens has many more innocent manifestations.   One of them is that which takes advantage of
the fact that Dickens happened to be a journalist by
trade.   It occupies itself therefore with hunting through
papers and magazines for unsigned articles which may
possibly be proved to be his.   Only a little time ago
one of these enthusiasts ran up to me, rubbing his
hands, and told me that he was sure he had found two
and a half short paragraphs in *All the Year Round*
which were certainly written by Dickens, whom he
called (I regret to say) the Master.   Something of this
archæological weakness must cling to all mere reprints
of his minor work.   He was a great novelist; but he was
also, among other things, a good journalist and a good
man.   It is often necessary for a good journalist to
write bad literature.   It is sometimes the first duty of
a good man to write it.   Pot-boilers to my feeling are
sacred things; but they may well be secret as well as
sacred, like the holy pot which it is their purpose to
boil.   In the collection called *Reprinted Pieces* there
are some, I think, which demand or deserve this
apology.   There are many which fall below the level
of his recognised books of fragments, such as *The*

Sketches by Boz, and *The Uncommercial Traveller*. Two or three elements in the compilation, however, make it quite essential to any solid appreciation of the author.

Of these the first in importance is that which comes last in order. I mean the three remarkable pamphlets upon the English Sunday, called *Sunday under Three Heads*. Here, at least, we find the eternal Dickens, though not the eternal Dickens of fiction. His other political and sociological suggestions in this volume are so far unimportant that they are incidental, and even personal. Any man might have formed Dickens's opinion about flogging for garrotters, and altered it afterwards. Any one might have come to Dickens's conclusion about model prisons, or to any other conclusion equally reasonable and unimportant. These things have no colour of the great man's character. But on the subject of the English Sunday he does stand for his own philosophy. He stands for a particular view, remote at present both from Liberals and Conservatives. He was, in a conscious sense, the first of its spokesmen. He was in every sense the last.

In his appeal for the pleasures of the people, Dickens has remained alone. The pleasures of the people have now no defender, Radical or Tory. The Tories despise the people. The Radicals despise the pleasures.

THE END